Wampus Cat Basketball History

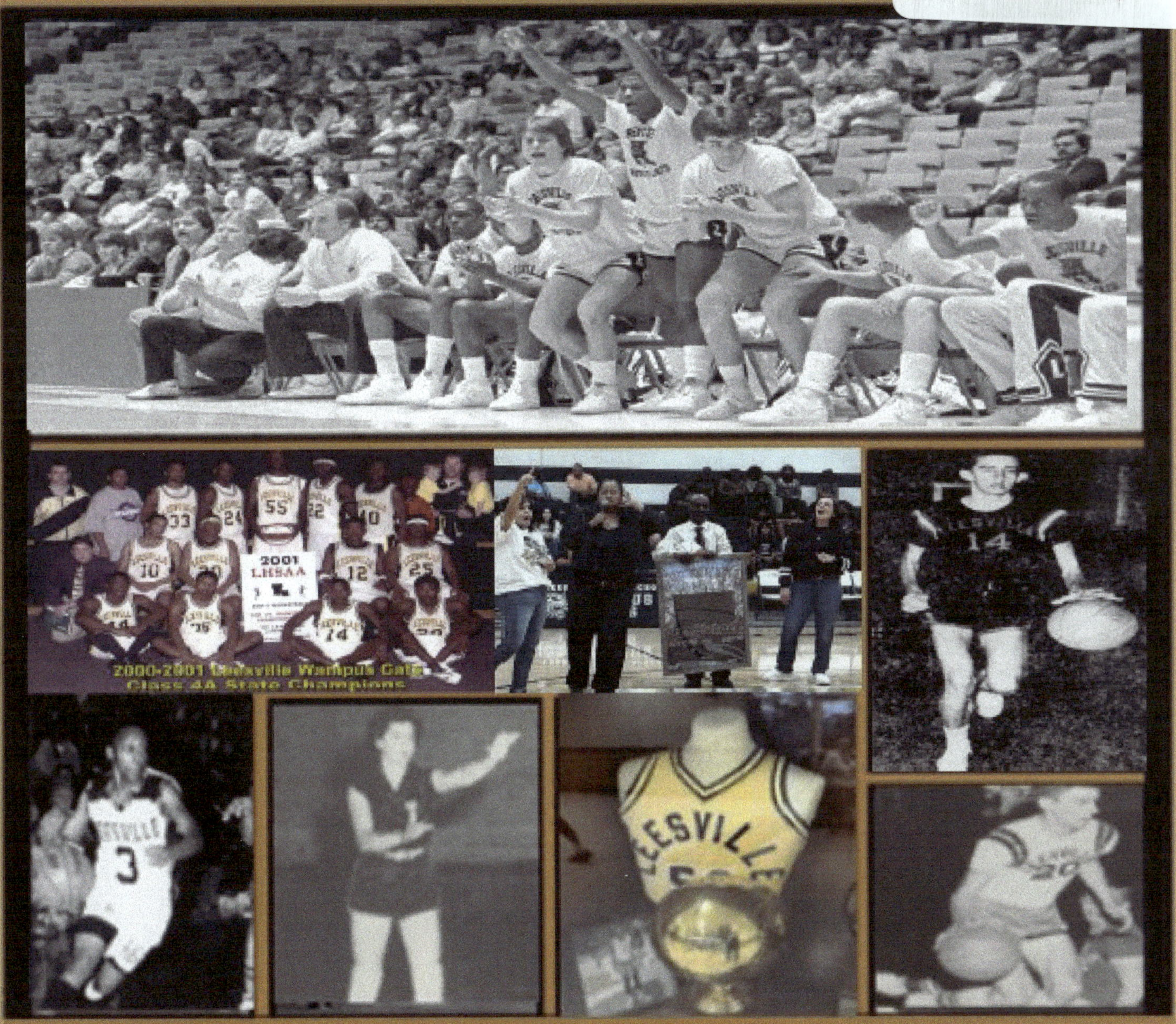

By Charles A. Owen & Billy Crawford

Published by the Reese Family of Vernon Parish

All Proceeds Go to LHS Basketball

Copyright, 2024

All Rights Reserved.

Table of Contents	iii
The Written History	1
Coaches at Leesville School	3
Year-by-Records	58
The Championship Season	73
Teams in Pictures	83
Scrapbook of Pictures, Box Scores and More	159
All State Selections	182
The Rich History of Leesville High School	186
LHS Sports Hall of Fame	188
Bonus Section: Other Champions at LHS	193
About The Authors	209
Sources and Methods	210
Index	211

The History of the Leesville High School Basketball
First Edition

By Charles A. Owen

With

Billy Crawford

This book chronicles the history of basketball at Leesville High School in Leesville, Louisiana. Without question, basketball has had the most success of any sport at Leesville High School. Both boys' and girls' teams have reached the State Finals on more than one occasion, with the 2001 boys winning the state championship.

Through the years, the Cats have won 18 district championship. The Lady Wampus Cats have 12. The boys' team has advanced to the state finals four times and the girls made it to the title game twice. The cagers from Leesville have made the state playoffs 60 times, with the boys garnering 40 of those spots and the girls achieving post season play 20 times.

This history book, like the History of Wampus Cat Football is an unofficial offering. There is no such thing as "official" histories of high school sports teams. There is no single place where all season, team and individual records are maintained. The Louisiana High School Athletic Association (LHSAA) does maintain lists of state champions and playoff actions and brackets through the years. A great group called 14-0 is slowly compiling results, titles and individual accolade lists through the years.

But, if an individual sport is going to be chronicled and a history is put together, the effort will be strictly organic and, in all likelihood, a volunteer effort.

The book you are reading is STRICTLY organic and fully a volunteer effort. The authors compiled this information through newspapers, yearbooks and to a small degree, via personal recollections. As you proceed through this document and find this holes in information and if you are in possession of any data that will help fill in holes or add to this work, please contact the authors.

In the ensuing pages, you'll see the history of both the boys' and girls' programs, broken down by decade. The intention is to present an historical narrative of each decade, highlighting seasons, titles won, playoff appearances and individual achievements.

The history presented here accurately reflects discoverable information since 1950. You'll see win/loss records by seasons, playoff appearances, All-District, All-State and All-American performers. When information is available (discoverable), you'll see scoring leaders for each year, as well. There is scant information available prior to 1950, and it will be presented in good faith, assuring anyone who views this document that this was all we could find.

NOTHING is hidden, nor intentionally NOT provided. If we could find it, we presented it.

You'll see a good number of pictures. Some are of high quality, and some are marginal. As stated earlier, if you have any additional information or pictures you can provide for this effort, PLEASE share them with the author. Most of the season-by-season data you see in this book is archived on the Facebook page called "History of Wampus Cat Basketball."

This book and subsequently the history of LHS basketball is told in terms of decades. While not a perfect way to analyze history, it is what we chose. Ideally, we would have liked to have gathered information from 1910 – forward, like the Wampus Cat Football History book. Sadly, access to and the availability of information prior to 1950 is inconsistent at best. Going forward from 1950, we have a pretty good handle on what happened. Prior to 1950, however, information appears in pockets.

The Written History
Pre-1950

The Great Game of Basketball: Some Quick History, by Billy Crawford

In 1891 James Naismith was a 31-year-old physical education instructor at the International YMCA Training School in Springfield, Massachusetts. He was tasked to create an indoor sport to keep the athletes indoors during harsh New England winters.

He nailed a peach basket on the wall 10 feet high. The game, named basketball, quickly grew and became very popular. Over the last 133 years there have been numerous changes in the rules- one thing has not: the basket's height is still 10 feet.

Senda Berenson, a physical education instructor at nearby Smith College, went to Naismith to learn more about the game. She adjusted several rules and formed a team.
Eleven months later she arranged the first official women's' basketball game played between Smith College and the University of California.

Naismith   Berenson

BASKETBALL IN LEESVILLE

The first year basketball is discovered in historical files is in 1913. An annotation from the local paper indicates that a team was fielded in 1913, and a number of players were listed. No record of any further activity was discovered in terms of wins and losses beyond this single annotation.

Boys' Basketball

This was the first year our boys have played basketball, and so a championship record could not be expected. Of four match games played one was won and three lost. The team, however, got some experience which will cause it to be heard from in the future. The players were as follows:

First Team.	Position.	Second Team.
McDaniel, captain	Right Guard	Smith
Averre	Left Guard	Lambreth
McAlpin	Right Forward	Gibbs
Davis	Left Forward	Free
Cudd	Center	Cavanaugh

The first year of recorded basketball activity is 1929. The Leesville Boys' team, coached by C.G. Stewart, defeated the DeRidder basketball team by a score of 25-22 in a game reported by the Leesville Leader. Sam Fertitta was high point man with 10 points. Jimmie Nichols and John Henry Gamblin followed with seven each. Red Beeson refereed to contest according to the Leesville Leader, Feb. 7, 1929. Fertitta and Beeson were focal points in the origins of football at Leesville, as well. Beeson coached and sponsored teams for LHS and Fertitta and his brothers were football stars. The Fertitta family were business leaders for many decades in Leesville, and Sam Fertitta served as a commissioned officer in the US Army in World War II.

The LHS Boys' team later attended the Natchitoches tournament. Coach C.G. Stewart's squad consisted of Sam Fertitta, Anthony Fertitta, Jimmie Nichols, Fred Rowzee, A. B. Cain, Jr. and Barney Cain.

Back in the early years of basketball few people in Vernon Parish had vehicles. Typically a coach or one player had a car so the team would load up and travel on Saturdays to play. Tournaments back then covered one day, starting early and playing late. Players and coaches would pack food and drinks for the team.

Basketball for girls first is noted at LHS in 1930. An 8 person squad is annotated in the pages of an LHS yearbook from that year. A number of local family names are easily identified in the first roster and as the coach.

LHS Girls' Basketball 1930

Back Row: Jeff Hicks, coach: Lana Cooley, Hollean Mathis, Denzel Smith, coach Austin Temple.
Front Row: Edith Bush, Adele Harville, Thelma Brogen, captain, Norma Wooley, Eunice Swain

1930 LEESVILLE BOYS' BASKETBALL

Back Row: "Five Seconds" Reid, Norris Bush, Peter Anderson, Homer Robinson, Kemp Tucker, Garland Stanley, Danny Ferguson, Jeff Hicks, coach.
Back Row: Ponder Craft, Clayton Lyons, Aubrey Bunch (captain), Finley Stanley, Milton Talbert

Vernon Parish Annual School Rally

During the 1930's most of the schools in Vernon Parish had a girls and boys basketball team. Each year the schools would travel to Leesville High, which was located "on the hill" on Texas Highway. Different events such as track and field and softball games were held at Gilbert Field, located down the hill from the Leesville School. Basketball was an integral component of the Rally and schools from around the parish competed against each other. During this same time period an outdoor dirt full-court basketball court was constructed for the basketball games. behind the school on the same as the present gymnasium.

In 1931, Leesville is credited with being the state runner up in boys' basketball. 14-0 Production reports that LHS was runner up to Dry Creek in Class 1A by a score of 45-39. Johnny Pelt was reported as the leading scorer and All-State performer for the Cats in a close-fought championship game.

Dry Creek Wins State Tourney
In Close Battle With Leesville

Teams which fought for first place in the final game of the recent Southwest Louisiana high school basketball tournament at the Southwestern Institute gymnasium, also met for honors in the state tourney at Baton Rouge Saturday, night, and history repeated itself when the Dry Creek boys came out victors over Leesville, as they did in the meet here.

The final scores in both games was close. In the state contest, Dry Creek had a final lead of 45 to 39, and in the district game here the count was 41 to 34.

BATON ROUGE, La., Mar. 9.—The Louisiana State High School Basketball Championship for 1931 today reposed with Dry Creek, whose gallant five defeated Leesville in the annual tournament finals here Saturday night, 45 to 39. The victory came in the closing minutes of play after Leesville had held an early lead.

Negreet took third place in the tournament by defeating Ponchatoula 50 to 30 in the consolation.

The Jena Giants, defending champions, were eliminated early in the tournament.

Roy Green, Dry Creek forward, was tournament high scorer with 68 points in four games. He was named on a mythical all-state tea malong with H. Weeks, Dry Creek, center; Beter, Jesuits guard; Johnny Pelt, Leesville, forward; and Fowler, Bolton, guard.

Not much information is available on a year to year basis for LHS basketball in the pre-1950s period. What we provide in these pages is probably representative of how things were through the 20s, 30s and 40s. The 1937 Basketball schedule for the aforementioned Vernon Parish rally is provided as an example of how things happened in those days.

Boys
Leesville vs. Hornbeck
Pitkin vs. Pickering
Orange (Anacoco) vs. Rosepine

Girls
Leesville vs. Evans
Pitkin vs. Pickering
Orange (Anacoco) vs. Simpson
Hornbeck vs. Rosepine

A search of archived yearbooks provides representative photos of boys' and girls' teams from the pre-1950 era

1947 LEESVILLE BASKETBALL TEAMS

Schedule

Ours			Theirs	
19	13	Pickering	9	14
7	2	Evans	18	9
9	15	Anacoco	13	7

Members

FIRST ROW
Dorothy Belle Roberts
Norma Chance
Helen Cooley
Hazel Pinchback

SECOND ROW
Helen Owens
Janice Haymon
Willie Mae Toney
Louise Jordan
Helen Rose
Betty Jean Hays
Lelia Lenahan

1947 Boys Basketball

SCHEDULE

Ours			Theirs		Members
2	14	Evans	20	16	Wayne Harper
18	8	Pickering	4	2	Bill Beavers
	28	Anacoco	32		Wayne Faulkner
	12	Simpson	19		Jimmy Rand
					J. C. Williams

1948 Teams

Top row, left to right: Delmon Craft, Sonny Nessmith, J. L. Smith, Larry Bailes, William Crews, Max Hill, James Williams, Bill Beavers.

Bottom row, left to right: Gayle Ellis, Roy Felt, Hubert Williams, B. A. Gill, James Bolgiano, Tommy Guess.

SCHEDULE

Leesville	7	Simpson	17
Leesville	2	Evans	18
Leesville	19	Evans	19
Leesville	24	Pickering	17
Leesville	29	Rosepine	7
Leesville	22	Rosepine	12
Leesville	11	Hornbeck	37
Leesville	12	DeRidder	24
Leesville	25	Pickering	29
Leesville	15	Leesville	21

Left to right: Ellen Cooley, Bonnie Ray Murphy, Norma Chance, Joy Ann Scogin, Billye Gregg, Helen Cooley, Hazel Pinchback, Betty Patty, Annette Norris, Georgia Faye Haymon.

SCHEDULE

Leesville	17	Evans	8
Leesville	14	Rosepine	11
Leesville	10	Evans	11
Leesville	5	Rosepine	11
Leesville	3	Hornbeck	26
Leesville	10	De Ridder	27
Leesville	10	Simpson	12

The 1950s

The Cats in the 50s were winners---by any measure. We can verify a record of 274 – 97 for the Wampus Cats and the Lady Cats have a discoverable record of 207-41. We say "discoverable" record because for some years, there is incomplete information available in terms of wins and losses.

For the boys in the 50s, two coaches led the Cats: Zolon Stiles and Billy Bennett. Coach Stiles, who was also the head football coach at LHS took the Cats to one state tournament (playoffs) in his 3 year tenure. Billy Bennett would become an institution at LHS and would establish himself as the all-time winner in basketball games until his record was eclipsed many years later by Hub Jordan.

In Bennett's 7 years at the helm in the 50s, the Cats won one district title and made the post season 5 times.

Dale Hardwick was one of the star players of the 1950s. Hardwick made All-State twice and averaged 22.3 points per game in his senior year. Other standout players in the 50s were Larry and Don Goins, Elber Sandell (All-State in 1953), Jimmy Edwards, Kennedy Smith, Louis Massie and JC Welch.

W. L. BENNETT
Coach

1958-59 Wampus Cats

DALE HARDWICK, Captain
Guard
All-District
All-State

The 1950s was the greatest decade in terms of team accomplishments for girls in LHS sports history. The Lady Wampus Cat basketball teams displayed dominance that has never been approached since those days.

In 1951, Coach AL Temple led the Lady Cats to a 42-7 record on the season and a runner up spot in the state tournament. In that great year, the Lady Cats lost to Oak Grove in the state finals (Girls Basketball (14-0productions.com)) Betty Paddy and Jane Carey was stars of the 1951 team.

In 1952, Guinnell Smart was named head coach and she guided the lady cagers to a record of 81-4 in 3 years. In 1952, the Lady Cats went 16-3 on the season and made it all the way to the state semi-finals. In 1953, the Cats went 36-1, advancing again to the state semi-finals. In 1954, the black and gold were state runner ups, and lost only one game---in the state finals against Winnsboro. Star players of this era were 3-time All-Stater Faye Jean, Gwendolyn Whittaker, Audrey Chamberlain and Shirley Cavanaugh.

FAYE JEANNE - All State
All State 1954

1954 Lady Wampus Cats, State Runner-Up, 29-1

In 1956 and 57, Coach Billy Bennett was a dual boys and girls coach. He achieved winning records and guided the Lady Cats to the State Semi-finals again. Agatha Rhodes was the head coach in 1958 and 59, but no season records, nor achievements could be found during research.

The 1960's: A Decade of Transition and a Lingering Question

The 1960s saw a lot of change for Wampus Cat basketball. For the boys, the Cats won more games than they lost, achieving a decade record of 290-138. For the girls, basketball disappeared, without fanfare and really without any historical rationale----at least not any that can be found via this research.

Billy Bennett remained at the helm and had 3 winning seasons in the 5 he coached for the Wampus Cats (60-64). Ralph Kees (65), Ed Young (66) Bobby Craft (67 and 68), and Jimmy Leach (69) all had brief stints as head coaches for the black and gold. For Bennett's tenure, the Cats saw some of the most prolific individual performances in school history. In 1961, Richard Reese would be named the State MVP in basketball. Reese set all sorts of school records and signed to play collegiately at Louisiana College, where he starred. After college, Reese returned to LHS as a coach, served later as principal and was eventually inducted into the LHS Sports Hall of Fame.

In 1964, Richard Schwartz set the school season-season scoring record with a 29.6 point per game average on the season. In the research completed for this book, Schwartz is the unquestioned single season scoring leader. Like Reese, Schwartz would also return to LHS, first serving as an Assistant Coach, then Head Coach for football. He served as Principal at Evans High School and later became Superintendent of Schools in Vernon Parish.

Richard Reese, Class of 61
All-State, 23.6 PPG

Richard Schwartz, Class of 64
All-State, 29.2 PPG

Final Wampus Cat Shooting Statistics

Name	Games	FGM	FG Av.	FTA	FTM	TP	Av.
R. Schwartz	23	285	40.8	140	106	676	29.3
B. Crawford	24	149	46.3	138	95	393	16.3
A. Temple	24	118	58.5	65	34	268	11.2
J. Henson	23	79	41.8	55	33	191	8.3
D. Phillips	23	44	46.8	39	26	114	4.8
J. Hengstenberg	22	15	44.4	3	2	32	1.5
J. Beltz	21	5	23.8	6	0	10	.5
J. Martinez	10	1	20.0	2	0	2	.2
B. Sexon	11	3	25.0	0	0	6	.5

Other key players in the first half of the 60s were Danny Hardwick, Bobby Craft, Edwin Cabra, Junior Temple and Billy Crawford.

In the second 5 years of the 1960s, the Cats had two winning seasons (65 and 69). Bobby Craft was hired literally right out of college and was the head coach in 67 and 68. Jimmy Leach led the Cats to a strong season in 1969, but no title was obtained, and no playoff berth was earned. Key players in these years were John Henson, Joe Gendron, James Latham, Tim Lynch, Vic Ortiz, Asa Skinner, Gary McDonald and Steve Laurence.

Edwin Cabra

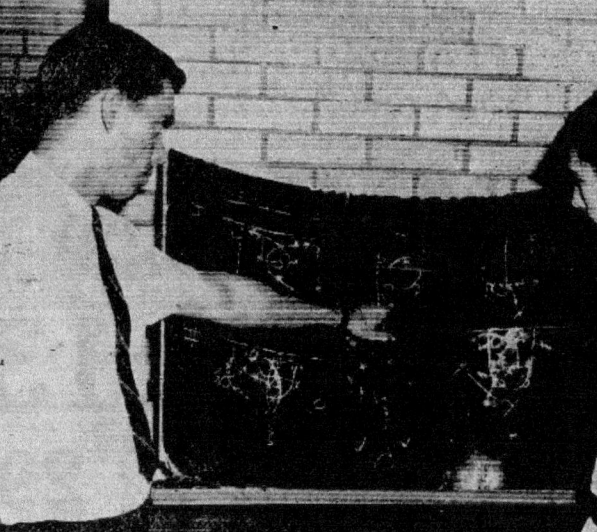

Coach Bobby Craft and Tim Lynch in 1967

Though winning seasons were achieved and some great individual performances were recorded during the 60s, the Cats did not make the postseason at all during the decade. In fairness, it should be pointed out that in those days, playoff appearances were very scarce---only the top 2 teams in each district would advance to the post-season. There was no such thing as Power Rankings and "wild card" entries.

Gary McDonald

L-R: Vic Ortiz, Coach Jimmy Leach, Asa Skinner

THE MYSTERY OF THE END OF GIRLS' BASKETBALL

Lady Wampus Cat basketball was discontinued after the 1961 season. Agatha Rhodes was the coach in 1960 and Vernia Gautreaux (later Lenahan) coached the squad in 1961. The 1960 squad posted a record of 10-14. Despite significant research, we could not find a final record for the 1961 team. We actually couldn't find many results at all. Key players for the 1961 team were identified as Colleen Young and Dorothy Davis. The 1961 yearbook did report that the Lady Cats won the Leesville Tournament, but no wins/losses could be found in media, nor in yearbooks.

The circumstances surrounding the end of girls' basketball are puzzling. Some students and faculty members from those days speculated that Leesville had a hard time scheduling teams and finding a district in which to compete. Some have speculated that the mores of the day locally drove the decision---to emphasize sports as a domain of male athletes.

1961 Girls' Team

There is no substantiation for either, but contrary facts exist that could refute either reason. Rural schools in Vernon Parish played girls basketball throughout the period of time the sport was disbanded at LHS. There were games that could be scheduled. Titles were won in all corners of the state in all classifications, as well. Research into the actual reasons for the end of girls basketball and all sports, in fact, continues.

In summary, from 1961 to 1975, there were no sports for girls at LHS. The reason behind this void remains a mystery. For some female athletes, other things were pursued. A family of female athletes was walking the halls of Leesville High in those days and they pursued a sport of their own---rodeo. Though LHS did not and still does sponsor the sport of rodeo, the achievements of the Porter girls' merits mentioning. Judy (Class of 1969), Cathy (1970) and Lindy (1975) were champions in the sport at state and national levels. One of the most successful athletes in those days and arguably LHS history was Judy Porter (later to become Weisgerber). Judy was a 4-year All-State selection in the sport of rodeo, as was her sister, Cathy. The girls were the daughters of National Rodeo, Louisiana Sports and LHS Hall of Famer T. Barett Porter.

July Porter   Lindy Porter

Societal Change: Integration and Black Athletes at LHS

Throughout the 1960s, the issue of segregation of the population by race simmered in all corners of the United States. The issue permeated all aspects of society, and schools were no exception. The deep south was especially affected by the situation because of the continuance of Jim Crow laws and the efforts to hang on to the ironic concept of "Separate But Equal" that festered across the south. History proved that Separate But Equal did not work and federal cases such as Brown v. Board of Education set the nation on the course of rectifying past wrongs, including in segregated schools.

The US government on a number of occasions in the 1960s had directed Vernon Parish to begin the process of integration but actions had been limited. Small numbers of Black students and faculty had been placed into Leesville schools and small numbers of Whites had been vectored to Vernon High and Elementary, but no wide-spread effort to integrate was made, nor visible.

In the Fall of 1969, Leesville's predominantly Black school, Vernon High and its associated elementary and middle schools were directed to be integrated into Leesville Schools. In effect, the high schools were merged into one, and Vernon's doors were closed and the population at Leesville High grew.

Black athletes were integrated first into practice with white athletes at LHS in the Fall of 1969. Robert Blow and Mose Tinsley, Jr were the first African American athletes at Leesville High School. Their presence would be felt immediately in the 1970 season.

The 1970s: Ups and Downs, Brushes with Greatness

The 1970s saw the Wampus Cats led by different coaches---all highly impactful. The black and gold achieved six winning seasons and garnered two district titles.

1962 graduate Richard Reese was hired as Head Coach in the fall of 1969 for the 1970 season. As mentioned previously, the first team at LHS to play in an integrated paradigm was the 69-70 team. Reese had been a highly successful player at Louisiana College and had taken a coaching position at Rapides High prior to coming back to Leesville.

The 1969-70 season saw both team and individual accomplishments. For the year, the Cats went 23-11 and finished tied for first in the District with Pineville. The black and gold earned a spot in the playoffs, but lost to DeRidder in the first round. Three athletes, Robert Blow, Gary McDonald and Steve Laurence earned All-District honors for the year. With Blow's selection, he became the first Black athlete at LHS to be named All-District in any sport. McDonald was a scoring powerhouse and on one occasion, dropped in 46 points in a single game---a record that remains to this date. Darren McQueen tied McDonald's record in 2013, but the mark has not been eclipsed at this writing.

Also of note for the 1970 season was Steve Laurence, who in addition to being a star basketball player was the Drum Major for the Wampus Cat band.

Robert Blow

Steve Laurence

Mose Tinsley Jr.

1971 and 1972 saw the Cats have back-to-back losing seasons, going 15-16 and 6-22, respectively. No athletes were named All-District in either season and no playoff appearances were earned.

From 1973 – 76, the Cats were led by Coach Keith Andrews. A graduate and All-State performer from East Beauregard, Andrews had played college basketball at Texas A&M and then McNeese and was a key cog in the Cowboys' 1968 NCAA Division II Playoff appearance. Andrews was a fiery coach and got the Cats on to a winning route immediately; the Cats had 3 winning seasons in the 4 with Andrews at the helm (20-15 in 73, 24-13 in 74, 30-7 in 75 and 16-19 in 76).

Stars from the mid 1970s were the Joiner brothers---John, Lawrence and Dennis---Deno Brown, Randall Smith, Raymond Smith, Dennis Mayeaux and Russell Murphy. The 1975 team did something no other boys' squad had done to this point---won the district title without losing any district games---going undefeated. The 1975 team won 30 games---a rare occurrence over the history of LHS basketball program. Coach Andrews won Coach of the Year awards in the 75 season, as well.

VARSITY: (L-r, top row), Head Basketball Coach Keith Andrews, Milton Clayton (mgr.), Brian Frederick (mgr.), Lawrence Joiner, John Joiner, Russell Murphy, Dexter Upshaw, Dennis Joiner, Sammy Bursh, Mike Boozer (mgr.), Robert Noel (mgr.), Assistant Coach Curtis Brazil. (Bottom row) Randall Smith, Deno Brown, Tracy Tinsley, Dennis Van Dine, Dennis Mayeaux, Raymond Smith.

Andrews was assisted primarily by a likeable and seasoned coach named Curtis Brazil. Coach Brazil had been a coach and principal at Pecan Island High School prior to coming to LHS in 1972. He was on-site at LHS until 1982 and was a beloved teacher and coach.

In 1977, LHS basketball was handed over to Michael Mallet as Head Coach. Mallet, a 1968 graduate of Vernon High School, was the first African American Head Coach at Leesville. His brother, Foster Thomas had served as an assistant coach right after integration, but Mallet was the first Black person to lead a team.

Michael Mallet had been an extraordinarily successful athlete at Vernon High, leading the Lions to two state football championships in the late 60s. He was also a multi-year letterman basketball player at Grambling prior to getting into high school coaching. He coached football and the freshman basketball team at LHS prior to taking on head coaching duties.

In the 77 and 78 seasons, the Cats had real success. Two players, Cedric Johnson and Jerry Lynch were scoring phenoms for the black in gold; both players earned All-District honors in both seasons. 77 and 78 both saw the Cats have winning seasons and earn post-season appearances. Other key players from those years were future LHS Principal and Superintendent of Schools James Williams, Robert Freshley, Dennis Joiner, Cordell Upshaw, Russell Murphy, Keith Joiner, James Rock and Gerald Kerry.

We're #1 — Standing L. to R. Coach Mallet, Ron Bouya, Richard Bastedo, Vernon Travis, Zeno Bursh, Robert Gaines, Mike McShane, Jerry Lynch, Robert Freshly, Cedric Johnson, Harold Tomas. Kneeling Jasper Keys, Rodney Simons, Gerald Kerry, Van Upshaw, James Rock, Jim Coburn, Keith Joiner, Steve Payton, Coach Culbreath.

Johnson and Lynch merit a brief paragraph of their own. Both were very good basketball players and played at the collegiate level (NSU for Lynch and Angelina Junior College for Johnson). But they were also history-making athletes in track and field. In 1978, Lynch was a 2 event All-State performer in the high jump and long jump. Johnson was a 5-time All-State athlete in hurdles and relays. Johnson, in fact, was an All-American in his senior year, leading an 880 (4 x 200) relay that broke the national, state composite, and AAA records in Louisiana. Johnson and Lynch were linchpins to the Wampus Cats' first team title in any sport in state track and field.

Jerry Lynch · Cedric Johnson

The Cats of 1979 had a down year. The team finished with a record of 9-17 and did not make the playoffs. No players were selected for the All-District squad.

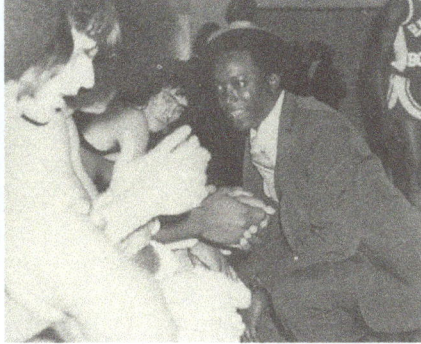

The Return of Girls' Basketball

In the fall of 1975, LHS fielded a girls' basketball team for the first time in 14 years. US law passed in the early 70s directed that female students would receive equal treatment as male students in all aspects of schooling---something that has been known as Title IX. This broad direction applied both to academic and athletic accommodations. With no female sports at all at LHS in 1975, LHS Principal, Dr. H. Lynn Russell made the decision to bring back sports for female athletes. No record of exists of actual court pressure to do this, however, the growing population of LHS, which included military family members who had played sports in other places and found themselves in Leesville with no options certainly helped prompt the action.

Russell hired a former LHS basketball star and young faculty member, Billy Crawford, to lead the first team. As a point of historical fact, there was really no such thing as youth sports in Leesville in those days, other than summer baseball and softball. Further, there was no junior high sports at all for girls (and there would not be any until the early 80s). The very idea of starting a varsity program from scratch with absolutely NO feeder programs or the existence of the sport in the general area was daunting at best.

Billy Crawford and an enthusiastic group of local and military female athletes pulled it off, almost in a shocking fashion. The Lady Cats burst on to the scene in varsity basketball after a 14 year hiatus and recorded a win/loss mark of 11-13. The daughter of one of LHS's most accomplished players and coaches, Ted Paris, was one of the foundations of Crawford's Lady Cats. Nita Paris earned All-District honors in her first year of organized basketball. The tenacious Paris teamed with Kathy Tinsley, Debbie Strait, and Donna Saunders in making an immediate splash back in LHS athletics.

1975-76 Lady Cats

L-R: Nita Paris MVP & Rebound Awards, Donna Saunders Coaches Award, Debbie Strait Scoring Award.
Nita graduated; Donna and Debbie were two outstanding sophomore guards. Their families were military —both moved at the end of the year.

Dr. HL Russell

The 1977 Lady Cats had a modicum of success, but the departure of 3 key players and the fact that no players were being developed locally in any fashion really made things difficult for the black and gold. The 77 team managed 6 wins, but 78 and 79 were lean years. Regardless, girls' sports were back at Leesville High School! Success was on the way.

1976-77 Lady Cats

Standing L-R: Coach Billy Crawford, Faye Windham, Debbie Crosby, Debbie Nix, Debra Cage, Valerie Peel, Kim Beavers, Carolyn Matthews, Linda Youngblood, Sandra Barnett, Cindy Broyles
Knelling: Angela Walker, Bonnie Hobbs, Barbara Moore, Karen Edwards, Kay Mayeaux, Penny Potter, Teola Crosby, Kathy Tinsley, Vicki West, Carolyn Moore.

Girls' Basketball — Susan Skidmore, Bonnie Hobbs, Pam Kennedy, Kathy Tinsley.

1979

The 80s: Big Years for the Wampus Cats

The decade of the 1980s saw some great basketball at LHS. The boys had 8 winning seasons in the decade and the girls team eclipsed the .500 mark 5 times.

In 1980, the Cats did struggle but they laid the foundation for years to come. In 1981, Coach Mallet's squad went 16-11 on the year and just making the LHSAA State Playoffs. Some of the key players from 1980 and 81 were Ketih Joiner (All-District), Vernon Travis, Levon White (All-District), Leon Jackson and Percy Gammage. Emerging during the 1981 season was a sophomore named Nikita Wilson, a tall and highly skilled athlete who had not played organized basketball prior to his 10th grade year.

Ready to roar onto the floor

Ready to roar out onto the floor preparatory to their game here last week against Jennings are, from left, Leon Jackson, Nikita Wilson, Levon White and Steve Kennedy. (Photo by Robert Chamberlain)

Leon Jackson & Levon White

Quick word on Levon White and Leon Jackson: Like Cedric Johnson and Jerry Lynch in 1978, White and Jackson were key components to a 1980 State Championship team---in track and field. White earned All-State honors in the 4 x 400 and 4 x 100 relays and Jackson picked up top 3 finishes in the high jump and triple jump. Section XX for a special section on the 78 and 80 track teams.

In 1982, the Cats went on fast forward and burst through the door of basketball elite. For the first time ever, the LHS cagers went through the season undefeated. Mike Mallet's team pulled off a 25-0 record on the season. Three Cats made All-District, including Nikita Wilson, Shelton Hickerson and Eric Travis. Coach Mallet was named Coach of the Year as the team made the post-season for the first time since 1978. Travis signed with Grambling and Hickerson signed to play with Angelina Junior College.

In 1983, the squad won the district again and compiled a record of 31-4. In the playoffs, LHS got its first post-season win since 1958 and advanced to the quarterfinals. Earning All-District honors for the year were Nikita Wilson (18.5 PPG), Steve Travis, Steve Kennedy and Grant Westerchil. Wilson would earn All-State and All-American honors on the season and would be one of the most highly recruited players in the country.

Rayne 4 12 26 35
Leesville 8 22 35 50
 Rayne — Jerold Taddio 8, Brad Hamn 19, Willie Cole 6, Carl Senegal 2.
 Leesville (31-3) — Steve Kennedy 12, Nikita Wilson 6, Eric Martin 7, Steve Travis 8, Randy Kennedy 6, Grant Westerchill 11.

Nikita Wilson   Steve Kennedy

Grant Westerchil   Steve Travis   Shelton Hickerson

Wilson signed with LSU and went on to a great career for the Tigers. After his senior year at LSU, he was drafted into the NBA by the Portland Trailblazers---making him the first Wampus Cat to be selected for the premier league on earth. Steve Kennedy signed to play at Tulsa University, where he lettered at the collegiate level, playing under the famed coach Nolan Richardson.

After the 83 season, Coach Mallet was hired for a position in athletics at LSU and subsequently, a new coach was named at LHS. Hubert Jordan assumed duties as head man at Leesville and began a tenure that would see him become the all-time winningest coach in Leesville history.

For the 84 season, Leesville had another winning campaign (17-12), but did not make the post season. Grant Westerchil and Randy Kennedy both earned All-District honors. Westerchil signed with McNeese State after his senior year and went on to earn a varsity letter for the Cowboys. Later in life, Nikita Wilson and Grant Westerchil were named to the LHS Sports Hall of Fame, as was 1960s star Richard Reese

Grant Westerchil, 2017
Basketball & Coaching

Nikita Wilson, 2022
Basketball

Richard Reese, 2014
Basketball & Coaching

In 1985, Coach Jordan led the Wampus Cats to heights not seen since the 1930s. On the season, Leesville went 29-6 and advanced all the way to the State Semi-Finals (Top 28 or "Final 4"). In the playoffs, the Cats defeated Port Allen, St. Thomas More and Alexandria Senior High before falling to Amite in the semis. Tony Marsh (18.1 PPG) and Darrell Jones earned All-District Honors for Leesville during the season.

TONY MARSH SHOOTS AGAINST DERIDDER DRAGONS

The Cats had winning seasons in 86 (16-13) and 87 (20-7), but did not win district, nor earn playoff berths. In 86, Michael Joiner and Anthony Burns both earned All-District honors. 86 grad Marro Hawkins would go on to sign with Centenary and earn multiple varsity letters and remains one fo the Gents' all-time leading scorers.

In 1987, All-District performers were Michael Joiner and Anthony Burns. Joiner's 25.5 Points Per Game Average earned him All-State honors in his senior year. Burns signed to play college basketball at Northeast Louisiana University (NLU)

In 1988, the Cats went 12-16. Robert Salisbury was named All-District.

In 1989, Coach Jordan's team once again ascended to the State Semi-Finals. LHS won the district for the first time since 1983 and placed 3 players on the All-District team, Robert Salisbury (17.8 PPG), Eric Rhodes, and Neal Travis. In the playoffs, the Cats defeated New Iberia, Robert. E. Lee, & Captain Shreve before falling to Shaw in the Final 4.

Lady Cats in the 80s

The early 80s saw some rough and ground breaking seasons for the Lady Wampus Cats. Sadly, no information can be discovered for wins and losses on the 1980 season. Kay Stephens coached the squad, but neither the LHS Yearbook nor any newspaper articles contained any final season standings. No one is recorded as being an All-District performer in the season. Pam Kennedy and Susan Scoggins were key players on the squad.

In 1981, the Lady Cats turned a corner. Though the team did not achieve a winning season, their record of 8-12 was respectable and the team was competitive all-year long. The squad was led by Regina Dixon and Monica Boerner, both scoring in double digits all-year long. Dixon made All-District on the season, averaging 17 points per game. Other key players on the squad included Kathy Ellis, Susan Scoggins, Regina Sparks and Tammy Kirk.

Regina Dixon | Susan Scoggins & Monica Boerner | Cathy Ellis

In 1982, Coach Mike Mallet took on the role of both boys' and girls' coach. Like Billy Bennett before him (in the late 50s), Mallet proved his mettle as a coach. As a reminder, in 1982, the boys' team went 25-1, running the table in the regular season. The girls under Mallet went 16-7 and tied for second in district, forcing a play-in game for the state playoff spot. The Lady Cats fell just short of a post-season birth, but success had returned to LHS. Monica Boerner and Regina Dixon both earned All-District honors in the 82 season. Boerner was offered a full scholarhsip to play at Lamar Univeristy. Dixon signed to play at Panola Junior College.

FIRST TEAM

Player, School	Ht.	Class	Avg.
Treasure Thomas, DeRidder	5-10	Sr.	15.3
Julie Fruge, Jennings	5-5	Sr.	10.5
Jill Knight, Jennings	5-9	Jr.	11.4
Regina Dixon, Leesville	5-6	Sr.	17.0
Monica Boerner, Leesville	5-10	Sr.	17.0

In 1983, the Lady Cats took a step backward, having a tough year at 3-18. The 83 season was the first year at LHS for Hubert "Hub" Jordan, who took on a one year assignment to coach the girls. In 1984, Coach Kay Taylor coached the girls to a 12-10 record and Connie Howard earned All-District honors. No playoff appearances were earned in 83 or 84

In 1985, Angela Self began a 3 year tenure as head coach. In her first year (1985), the Lady Cats finished with a winning record of 17-12. The Lady Wampus Cats fell just short of a playoff appearance but were in contention until the last week. Ginny Freshley, Lorenda Smart and Kim Dowden were key players on the squad.

In 86 and 87, the Lady Cats went 6-16 and 15-15. No playoff appearances were earned no district titles were won. Ginny Freshley earned All-District honors in 1987 and went on to a successful career playing at Louisiana College (now Louisiana Christian University).

1987 Lady Cats   Yvette Borrero   Ginny Freshley

In 1988, LHS hired Louise "Do" Bonin as Head Coach. Bonin would have six years at the helm and guide the Lady Wampus Cats to their highest finish in school history since the 1950s and stands to this day as the most accomplished squad since basketball was re-started in 1975. The 1988 squad went 17-10 and Melissa Cleary made All-District. In 1989, the team went 18-10 and earned a spot in the LHSAA State Playoffs. LHS defeated Ruston in the first round of the playoffs and lost to Natchitoches in the second round. The win versus Ruston was Leesville's first post-season game or win since 1957. Angie Thomas was named District MPV (13.8 PPG) as was Karen Howard.

Karen Howard & Trivia Horner   Angie Thomas   Kim Brown

1988 Lady Wampus Cats

The 1990's: Wampus Cats in Contention

The 1990s saw some big days for the Cats and Lady Wampus Cats.

For the boys, Hub Jordan finished out his last five yeas as head coach. For his five years at the helm in the 90s, Jordan guided the Cats to a record 118 – 41. Cumulatively, for his career as a boys' head coach, Jordan's record stands at 241-104, the most in LHS history. In 1990 the Cats went 27-7 season and made it to the first round of the playoffs. Miguel Yepez, an exchange student from Brazil (??) earned All-District honors.

Miguel Yepez   Zack White   Patrick Kennedy

In 1992, LHS went 25-10 and won the district outright. In the playoffs, the Cats defeated Northside in first round of the LHSAA tournament but lost in the 2nd round to Capitol High of Baton Rouge. Patrick Kennedy (MVP, 25.2 PPG), Ennis Flowers and Scott Larue all earned All-District honors. Kennedy earned All-State honors on the season, as well.

In 1993, Leesville record would stay on the winning track, going 20-10 on the season. The Cats tied for 2nd in district and had to into a play-in game to obtain a spot in the LHSAA tournament. The Cats lost to LaGrange and missed the playoffs. Ennis Flowers earned All-District for the season. In 1994, in Jordan's last year, Leesville went 25-8 and tied Washington-Marion for first place in district. The Cats won their first round vs Wossman but were upended by Glen Oaks in the 2nd round. Ronnie DeGray (17 PPG), Demond Mallet and Montrel Dorsey earned All-District honors and DeGray signed to play collegiately with Howard College and later transferred to the University of Colorado.

Montreal Dorsey   Chad Clark   Demond Mallet

In 1994, former LHS player Grant Westerchil was hired as Head Coach for the Wampus Cats. Grant had a great playing career at LHS and in college. He was also the son of a successful coach and former principal (at several schools), Joe Westerchil. Grant went immediately to work and kept the Cats on a winning track in the 1995 season. Leesville went 21-10 on the season, winning the district and running the table without a defeat. In the playoffs, the Cats lost in the first round. Demond Mallet (22 PPG), Reggie DeGray and Lonnie Thomas all were named All-District on the season and Westerchil was named Coach of the Year.

In 1996, the Cats had a season for the record books. The black and gold went 27-8 for the year and made it to the State Finals, losing a heart breaker to Cohen of New Orleans in the championship game. Leesville defeated Tioga, Carroll (quarterfinals) and St. Thomas More along their path to the title game. Demond Mallet (MVP, 27.6 PPG) made All-State for the season and recorded the second-best single-season performer of any Wampus Cat; Mallet was named State MVP and signed with McNeese State and had a sterling college and pro basketball career playing in Europe. Reggie DeGray earned All-State honors and played collegiately at Wofford University and later Louisiana-Lafayette. Lonnie Thomas was selected All-District and Westerchil was named District Coach of the Year.

In 2021, Demond Mallet joined Richard Reese, Coach Westerchil and Richard Reese in the LHS Sports Hall of Fame.

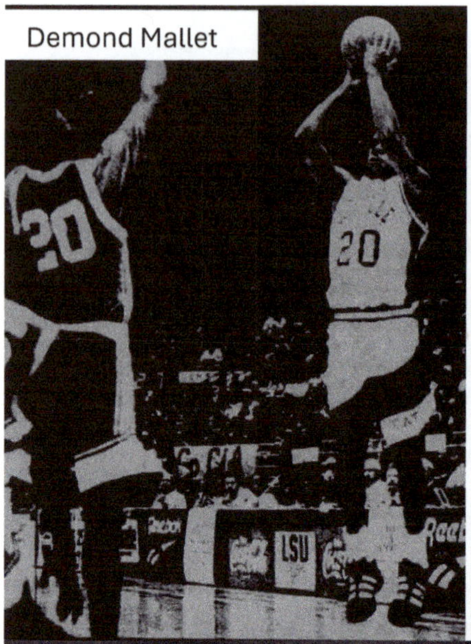
Demond Mallet

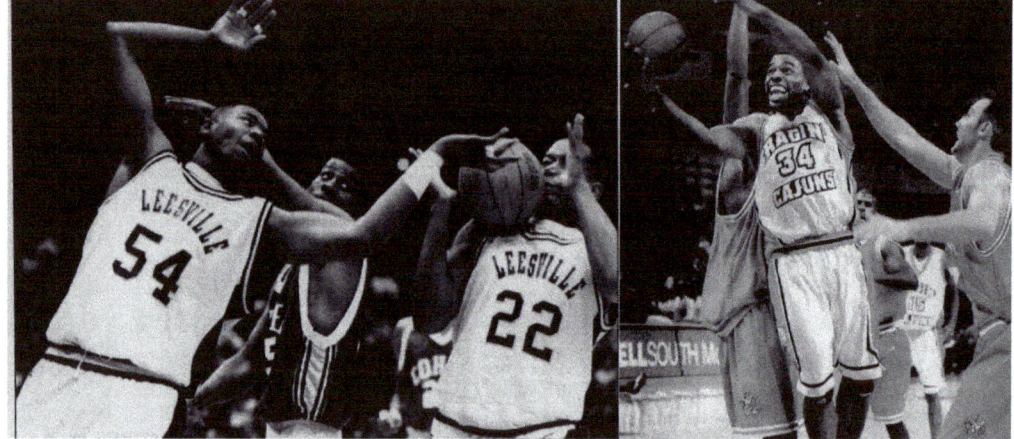

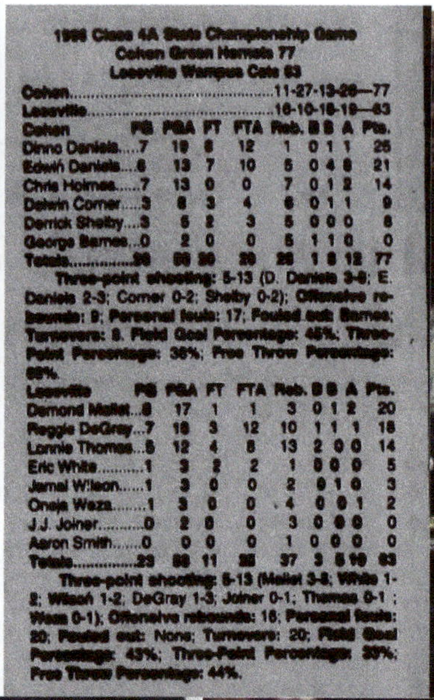

1996 Class 4A State Championship Game
Cohen Green Hornets 77
Leesville Wampus Cats 63

Cohen	11-27-13-26—77
Leesville	16-10-18-19—63

Cohen	FG	FGA	FT	FTA	Reb.	B	S	A	Pts.
Dinno Daniels	7	19	8	12	1	0	1	1	25
Edwin Daniels	6	13	7	10	5	0	4	8	21
Chris Holmes	7	13	0	0	7	0	1	2	14
Delwin Corner	3	8	3	4	6	0	1	1	9
Derrick Shelby	3	5	2	3	5	0	0	0	8
George Barnes	0	2	0	0	5	1	1	0	0
Totals	26	60	20	29	26	1	8	12	77

Three-point shooting: 5-13 (D. Daniels 3-8; E. Daniels 2-3; Corner 0-2; Shelby 0-2); Offensive rebounds: 9; Personal fouls: 17; Fouled out: Barnes; Turnovers: 8. Field Goal Percentage: 45%; Three-Point Percentage: 38%; Free Throw Percentage: 69%.

Leesville	FG	FGA	FT	FTA	Reb.	B	S	A	Pts.
Demond Mallet	8	17	1	1	3	0	1	2	20
Reggie DeGray	7	18	3	12	10	1	1	1	18
Lonnie Thomas	5	12	4	8	13	2	0	0	14
Eric White	1	3	2	2	1	0	0	0	5
Jamal Wilson	1	3	0	0	2	0	1	0	3
Oneja Weza	1	3	0	0	4	0	0	1	2
J.J. Joiner	0	2	0	0	3	0	0	0	0
Aaron Smith	0	0	0	0	1	0	0	0	0
Totals	23	58	11	25	37	3	5	10	63

Three-point shooting: 6-13 (Mallet 3-8; White 1-2; Wilson 1-2; DeGray 1-3; Joiner 0-1; Thomas 0-1 ; Weza 0-1); Offensive rebounds: 16; Personal fouls: 20; Fouled out: None; Turnovers: 20; Field Goal Percentage: 43%; Three-Point Percentage: 30%; Free Throw Percentage: 44%.

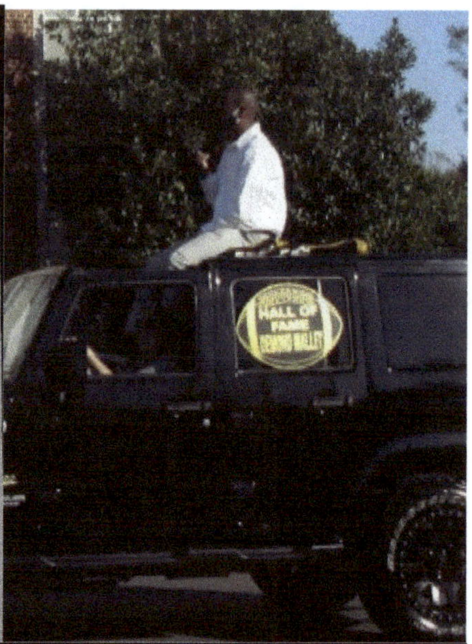

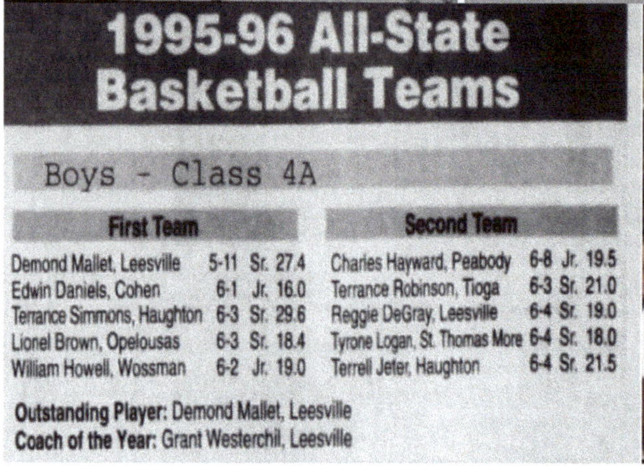

1995-96 All-State Basketball Teams

Boys - Class 4A

First Team				Second Team			
Demond Mallet, Leesville	5-11	Sr.	27.4	Charles Hayward, Peabody	6-8	Jr.	19.5
Edwin Daniels, Cohen	6-1	Jr.	16.0	Terrance Robinson, Tioga	6-3	Sr.	21.0
Terrance Simmons, Haughton	6-3	Sr.	29.6	Reggie DeGray, Leesville	6-4	Sr.	19.0
Lionel Brown, Opelousas	6-3	Sr.	18.4	Tyrone Logan, St. Thomas More	6-4	Sr.	18.0
William Howell, Wossman	6-2	Jr.	19.0	Terrell Jeter, Haughton	6-4	Sr.	21.5

Outstanding Player: Demond Mallet, Leesville
Coach of the Year: Grant Westerchil, Leesville

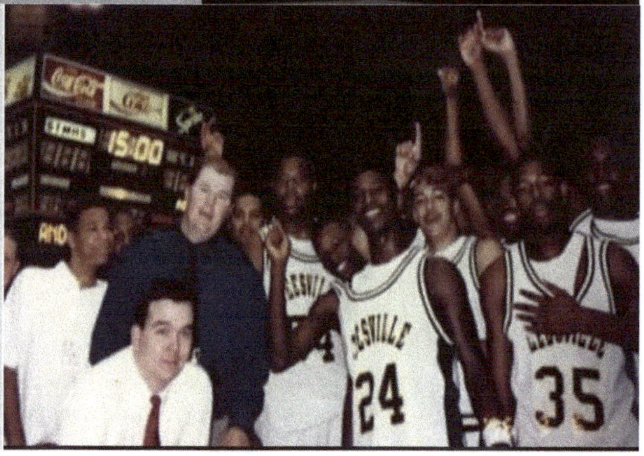

Lonnie Thomas & Aaron Smith

Reggie DeGray

In 1997, the Cats had another willing season, going 25-9 on the year and repeating as district champions. In the playoffs, LHS defeated Haughton in the first round but fell to the defending champion, Cohen in the second round. JJ Joiner and Jamal Wilson earned All-District honors for the

season. In 1998, LHS again finished first in the district (tied with Eunice) and again made it to the playoffs, advancing to the second round of the state tournament. JJ Joiner (Dist MVP/19.5 PPG), Jeff Brown, and Derek Wright earned All-District honors on the year.

Jeffrey Brown

JJ Joiner

Jamal Wilson

In 1999, the Cats closed out the decade with another big season, winning 27 and losing only 7 games on the season. In the playoffs, Leesville defeated Bishop Sullivan in the opening round and lost to Baker in the second (regional) round of the playoffs. Derek Wright and Darnell Bradley earned All-District honors. Wright was also named to the All-State team

1998-99 4-4A Boys All-District Basketball Team

FIRST TEAM

Name, school	Cl	Avg
Derrick Wright, Leesville	Sr.	23.5
Brannon Barfield, Sam Houston	Jr.	16.0
Darnell Bradley, Leesville	Jr.	16.0
Nick Dugas, Crowley	Sr.	17.0
Josh Thibodeaux, Eunice	So.	20.0

Lady Cats in the 1990s

The 1990 season saw the Lady Wampus Cats take a step backwards after their successful 89 campaign. Coach Bonin's squad went 10-18 for the years. No district title was won, nor was a playoff spot in the offing. Tangie Riley did make the All-District team, however.

In 1991, the Lady Wampus Cats had the best and most successful season of any LHS girls' basketball team since the 1950s. The ladies in black and gold went 25-7 on the season and advanced to the LHSAA State Quarterfinals. The Cats won their district and earned a first-round bye in the playoffs; in the second round, they defeated East Ascension and advanced to the quarterfinals. Tangie Riley, Carissa Badger and Tiffany Clifton made All-District. Coach Bonin was named District Coach of the Year.

1991 Lady Wampus Cats, State Quarterfinalists

The 1992 Lady Cats finished the season with a 20-8 record and in a 3-way tie for first place--- a good season! They lost a play-in game for the official district title, but made the playoffs. Coach

Bonin's squad lost the first round of the playoffs to Comeaux. Tiffy Clifton, Tracy Thomas and Joye Pangelinan were named to the All-District team. Clifton and Thomas both signed National Letters of Intent to play for Tulane in their senior season.

In 1993, the Lady Cats again achieved a winning season, finishing 20-13. Coach Bonin's team earned a berth in the state playoffs and won a first-round game at West Monroe. Byrd knocked the Cats out of the playoffs in the second round. Tiffany Clifton and Tracey Thomas repeated as All-District performers on the season. It should be noted that Leesville played in 5A for a period of time in the early 90s, which made competing in all sports more difficult. The Lady Cats remained competitive through this period, however. The Cats lost Louise Bonin after the season. LHS's head coach decided to go back to college for a sabbatical and to pursue a master's degree. In the history of LHS, Coach Bonin holds an important place in the contest of girls' basketball---she should be credited with bringing on a consistent period of winning and competitiveness.

The 1994 Lady Cats completed their season with a 13-15 mark. They were in the playoff hunt until the final game of the season (in 2nd place with a game to go), but the ball didn't bounce their way. Sherry Broocks took over as the coach for the year; Mary McChrystal and Tori Daniel were named All-District on the season.

In the summer of 1995, LHS hired a new girls' basketball coach----Joe Sowells. Coach Sowells immediately went about winning and the Lady Cats went 20-12 in his first season. Leesville won its district and notched a playoff win. The Lady Cats defeated Glen Oaks in the first round and fell short to Opelousas in the 2nd round. Tori Daniels (12 PPG), Cornelia Miller and Nikki Hiers all made All-District and Coach Sowells was named Coach of the Year for the district. Daniels signed to play collegiately with Louisiana College after her senior year.

Cornelia Miller   Nya Wilson   Joe Sowells   Eula Hickman

    In 1996, the Lady Cats went 17-12 on the season. Coach Joe Sowell's team won their district and made a playoff appearance. Leesville lost its first-round playoff game to Walker. Key players on the team were Angela Davidson (14 PPG) and Kurtina Holland. Davidson, like Tangie Riley, would make All-District 3 years in a row. More to follow on her high school and collegiate career in future posts. In 1997, In 1997, the Lady Cats won their district AGAIN, finishing the season with a 19-9 record. All district performers on the season were Angela Davidson and Viola Thomas. Coach Joe Sowells was named Coach of the Year. As district champs, the Lady Cat made the state playoffs but went out in the first round in a tough loss to Marksville.

1997 4-4A ALL-DISTRICT

First Team

NAME	HT.	CLASS	AVG.	SCHOOL
Melanie Vidrine	5'8"	Jr.	11.0	Sam Houston
Hope Sinclair	5'6"	Jr.	14.0	Crowley
Nevia Marks	5'10"	Jr.	14.0	DeRidder
Sonya Williams	5'9"	Jr.	11.0	Wash./Marion
Angela Davidson	5'10"	Jr.	18.2	Leesville

Outstanding Player - Angela Davidson - Leesville
Coach of the Year - Joe Sowells - Leesville

Second Team

NAME	HT.	CLASS	AVG.	SCHOOL
Shanel Handy	5'3"	So.	13.3	DeRidder
Kena Clay	5'5"	Sr.	5.6	Crowley
Kivoli Thomas	6'0"	Jr.	9.5	Wash./Marion
Viola Thomas	5'9"	So.	12.4	Leesville
Sarah Masters	5'11"	Sr.	14.0	DeRidder

Kena Clay

The Lady Cats won the district again in 1998, finishing the season with a 17-11 record. The squad landed two athletes on the All-District team---Viola Thomas and Angela Davidson. Davidson was also named First Team All-State and averaged 22 points per game in her senior year. After high school, Angela played a full career at the collegiate level---two years at Ole Miss and two years at Northwestern State. Davidson went to great success at NSU, meaning All-Conference honors and later being named to the university's Hall of Fame.

1997-98 LSWA Class 4A All-State Basketball Team

Girls' First Team

Player	School	Ht.	Class	PPG
Kisha James	Pineville	5-6	Sr.	33.0
Angela Davidson	Leesville	5-11	Sr.	22.0
Shondra Johnson	St. Mary's	5-9	Sr.	30.9
Jamie Thomatis	Ursuline	5-11	Sr.	27.6
Selena Businelle	Assumption	6-1	Sr.	15.6

Angela Davidson | Ebony Parker & Sheronda Bowers

in 1999 the Lady Wampus Cats had a great regular season---winning the district and notching 22 wins. The Lady Cats had a brief playoff run, however, and were eliminated in the first round by Bastrop. All-District performers in the season were Sheronda Bowers, Viola Thomas; and Sepi Toga;. Coach Sowells was named district Coach of the Year. Bowers, would earn All-District honors for 3 years, poured in 18 points a game for the year. Viola Thomas picked up her second stanza of All-District accolades.

The 2000s: Decade For a Title

In 2000, the Wampus Cats made another trip to the state championship game under Coach Grant Westerchil. The boys' squad won the district title and went 33-5, achieving the highest number of wins in school history. In the playoffs, the Cats defeated Bossier in the first round, Lee High (Baton Rouge---now Liberty High) in the second round, Parkway in the quarterfinals and Salmen in the Semi-finals. LHS fell to basketball powerhouse Peabody and LHSAA and Louisiana State Hall of Fame Coach Charles Smith in a tough loss in the title game. Individually, Darnell Bradley (19.8 PPG), Eric Woods and Chris Campbell earned All-District honors. Bradley was named to the All-State team and signed to play collegiately with Northwestern State. Coach Westerchil was named 4A State Coach of the Year, as well.

Darnell Bradley—All-State

Coaches Reese & Westerchil, & Darnell Ball

Class 4A
Leesville 78, Salmen 75

LEESVILLE (33-4)
Ball 0-0 2-4 2, Woods 5-8 4-4 15, Campbell 2-4 6-10 10, Long 5-7 9-10 20, Hawkins 0-2 0-0 0, Scott 3-8 3-5 9, Bradley 7-9 7-7 21. Totals 22-38 31-40 78.
SALMEN (30-6)
Carlin 1-6 0-0 3, Martin 0-2 0-0 0, Monahan 0-0 0-0 0, Edwards 6-13 2-3 17, Duhon 7-16 1-2 17, Mills 0-0 0-0 0, Kelly 0-1 0-0 0, Smith 5-15 8-12 20, Buckley 8-10 0-0 20, Abadie 0-0 0-0 0. Totals 28-63 11-17 75.
Leesville   25 15 14 24–78
Salmen   18   9 19 29–75
3-Point goals—Leesville 3-7 (Woods 2-3, Long 1-2, Scott 0-2), Salmen 8-24 (Edwards 3-5, Smith 2-5, Duhon 2-8, Carlin 1-3, Martin 0-2, Kelly 0-1). Fouled out—Bradley, Martin, Duhon, Mills, Buckley. Rebounds—Leesville 35 (Scott 8), Salmen 20 (Buckley 10). Assists—Leesville 13 (Woods, Bradley 4), Salmen 12 (Duhon 5). Total fouls—Leesville 15, Salmen 29. Turnovers—Leesville 30, Salmen 18. A—na.

1999-2000 District 4-4A
All-District Basketball Teams

Boys' First Team

Player	School	Class	PPG
Joshua Thibodeaux	Eunice	Jr.	31.0
Darnell Bradley	Leesville	Sr.	18.1
Brannon Barfield	Sam Houston	Sr.	17.8
Joseph Guilbeau	Washington-Marion	Sr.	14.8
Cedric Scott	DeRidder	Sr.	16.1

Boys' Second Team

Player	School	Class	PPG
David Carpenter	Sam Houston	Sr.	19.0
Eric Woods	Leesville	Soph.	12.7
Anthony Johnson	Washington-Marion	Jr.	14.1
Jordan Sonnier	DeRidder	Sr.	13.8
Chris Campbell	Leesville	Jr.	14.4

Most Valuable Player: Joshua Thibodeaux, Eunice
Coach of the Year: Grant Westerchil, Leesville

Honorable Mention

Nick Guidry, Washington-Marion; Kellen Wright, Washington-Marion; Justin Joseph, Washington-Marion; Casey Long, Leesville; Naquan Larue, Eunice; Lloyd Jones, Crowley.

2001: The Championship Season

While all seasons are important and all history should be reported within bounds of space and information that is discoverable, the 2001 season stands out and merits special attention in this book. The 2001 Wampus Cat boys' team achieved something no other basketball team at Leesville ever accomplished and, in truth, only two other teams in the entire history of LHS athletics---they won a state championship. The 2001 squad finished the unfinished business of 1996 and 2000 when the Cats made it to the state title game but fell just short of the title. Grant Westerchil's team in 2001 stands alone as state title winners.

The squad finished the season with a sterling record of 28-8 and won their district outright. Eric Woods (21.8 PPG), Chris Campbell and Marcus Johnson were named to the All-District team. Woods was also named First Team All-State and went on to play collegiately and letter in multiple seasons at Louisiana Tech and Northwestern State. In the playoffs, Leesville defeated Scotlandville in the first round, Salmen (Slidell) in the second round, St Thomas Moore in the quarterfinals and Carver (New Orleans) in the semi-finals.

In the championship, the Cats defeated Woodlawn of Baton Rouge by a score of 74-65. The article from the game in the Leesville Leader provides the best narrative of the game. Special thanks to Daniel Green for his consistent reporting over many years.

Jonathan Hopkins   Eric Woods   Grant Westerchil

Cats defeat Woodlawn in 4A title game

By Daniel Green
Sports Editor

LAFAYETTE — Finally.

After five appearances in the Top 28, the Leesville Wampus Cats captured a state basketball title, defeating the Woodlawn Panthers 74-65 Saturday night in the Cajundome.

"This feels a whole lot better than finishing second," said Leesville head coach Grant Westerchil. "We have worked so hard to get to this point. I am just so proud of these guys. They are special."

Leesville (28-8) concluded the season on a 16-game winning streak, brining home their first state championship to the school since 1978's track championship.

The Cats fell behind 3-0 when Landon Snoddy hit a three 13 seconds into the game. However, Eric Woods hit two free throws and a layup over the next two minutes to put Leesville in the driver's seat, 11-3.

Leesville eventually moved out to an 11-point edge at 19-8 on a shot by Chris Campbell. But James Collins hit a three-pointer and Kendrick Barber hit a jumper to pull the Panthers to within six points, 19-13.

Woodlawn cut the deficit to four points on three occasions during the second quarter, the last time at 26-22. But Marcus Johnson hit a three-pointer to stem the tide and Woods followed with another triple to help the Cats take a 32-27 lead into the intermission.

"I felt that we were in pretty good shape at the half," said Woodlawn head coach Kenny Almond. "But it seemed to me that Leesville was more determined than we were."

However, it looked as if Woodlawn might get it going as Jerimie Coller lit up the scoreboard for 15 points in the third quarter. But Leesville managed to maintain the lead, using a 22-20 advantage to move out to a 54-47 lead going into the final eight minutes.

Woodlawn chipped the lead down to 58-54 with a 7-4 run. But the Cats sealed the win on the free throw line, connecting on 10-of-15 attempts down the stretch to take the victory.

"When you can hit your free throws, it makes you very hard to beat," Westerchil said. "We have hit our free throws during the playoffs and we did it again tonight."

For the game, the Cats hit 20-of 26 foul shots, including 11-of-11 from Campbell, who had 28 points to lead Leesville.

Woods came in with 22 points and 10 rebounds to capture game MVP honors. Johnson added 17 points and six rebounds.

Collier and Collins each had 17 points in the loss for the Panthers while Barker had 13 points.

Chris Campbell

Prep Top 28
4-A Championship
Leesville 74, Woodlawn 65

LEESVILLE (28-8)
Eric Woods 8-20 2-4 22, Chris Campbell 8-11 11-11 28, Jonathan Hopkins 0-1 0-1 0, Marcus Johnson 5-7 6-8 17, James Carter 0-2 0-0 0, Johnnie Hearns 0-3 1-2 1, Chris Elkins 0-0 0-0 0, Gabe Wilson 0-0 0-0 0, Walter Mason 0-1 0-0 0, Dennis Joiner 0-0 0-0 0, Onterrio Agnew 0-0 0-0 0, Aaron Moore 3-8 0-0 6, Sam Burley 0-0 0-0 0. **Totals 24-53 20-26 74.**
WOODLAWN (34-4)
James Collins 3-11 9-14 17, Shaun Ray 2-4 0-0 5, Karandick Ogunride 1-4 0-0 2, Darnell Lazare 1-4 2-3 4, Landon Snoddy 1-3 0-0 3, Ledell Eackles 0-0 0-0 0, Jacob Triche 2-2 0-0 4, Lance Coleman 0-2 0-0 0, Kendrick Barber 4-9 4-8 13, Kendrick Knighten 0-0 0-0 0, Jerimie Colllier 6-12 3-3 17. **Totals 20-51 18-28 65.**

Leesville	19	13	22	20—74
Woodlawn	13	14	20	18—65

Three-point goals—Leesville 6-16 (Woods 4-8, Campbell 1-2, Johnson 1-2, Hopkins 0-1, Hearns 0-3), Woodlawn 7-20 (Collins 2-7, Collier 2-6, Ray 1-2, Snoddy 1-2, Barber 1-2, Coleman 0-1). **Fouled out**—Campbell. **Rebounds**—Leesville 35 (Woods 10), Woodlawn 32 (Barber 7). **Assists**—Leesville 7 (Johnson 3), Woodlawn 11 (Ray 6). **Total fouls**—Leesville 22, Woodlawn 20. A—NA.

4-4A All-District boys

FIRST TEAM

Name, school	Cl.	Ht.	Avg.
Josh Thibodeaux, Eunice	Sr	6-2	29.5
Eric Woods, Leesville	Jr	6-3	21.0
Anthony Johnson, Wash-Marion	Sr	6-2	13.6
Chris Campbell, Leesville	Sr	6-2	17.0
Andre Herron, DeRidder	Sr	6-0	14.3

Second Team

Name, school	Cl.	Ht.	Avg.
Jeff Jones, DeRidder	Sr	6-3	17.4
Marcus Johnson, Leesville	Jr	6-2	14.5
Bryce DeJean, Crowley	Jr	6-1	14.4
Chris Phillips, Wash-Marion	Jr	6-3	12.5
Kyle Savant, Eunice	Sr	6-3	10.0

MOST VALUABLE PLAYER
Josh Thibodeaux, Eunice
COACH OF THE YEAR
Grant Westerchil, Leesville

LSWA 4A All-State Team

BOYS
First Team

Name, School	Ht	Cl	Avg
Darrel Mitchell, St. Martinville	5-11	Jr	21.0
James Collins, Woodlawn	6-1	Jr	19.5
Josh Thibodeaux, Eunice	6-2	Sr	29.5
Eric Woods, Leesville	6-3	Jr	21.0
Bryan Rusley, B.T. Washington	6-2	Sr	23.1

Coach Westerchil resigned his post as Head Basketball Coach after the state title game. In 7 years as the Cats' head coach, Westerchil compiled a record of 179-55, notching a winning percentage of .76, the highest in LHS history. Though several men have more wins as head coach (i.e. Hub Jordan and Billy Bennett), Westerchil had the highest winning percentage and was the most successful in terms of post-season play. Replacing Grant on the bench was the son of a former LHS coach and player. Tracy Reese, the son of Richard, had been an assistant for Westerchil and ramped up as head signal caller almost immediately after the end of the season.

In 2002, the Cats went 20-10 on the season and made another trip the post season. Leesville knocked off Bastrop in the first round of the playoffs but fell to St. Martinville in the regional round. All District performers for the year were Eric Woods (17.8 PPG) and Marcus Johnson. Woods repeated as an All-State selection and went on to play collegiately for a full career in Ruston and Natchitoches.

Marcus Johnson   Eric Woods

In 2003, the Cats kept winning. The final record for the year was 20-11 with a trip to the playoffs. All-District performers for the year were Daryl Joiner and Frank Larry. In 2004, Coach Reese's squad finished 23-11 and also made a trip to the playoffs, but went out in the first round with a loss to Istrouma. Frank Larry and Terrance Blake were named to the All-District team for the season.

Daryl Joiner   Frank Larry   Marcus Singleton

In 2005, the Cats had yet another winning season, going 27-7 on the campaign. Coach Reese's squad tied for first in district with Peabody of Alexandria. The Wampus Cats fielded one of its most talented teams ever, with Daryl Joiner, Frank Larry and Terrance Blake leading the charge. Also contributing big things in the 2005 season was Chris Watson. As a district champ always does, the Cats earned a spot in the playoffs, but were eliminated in the first round by Opelouss. Larry, Blake and Joiner earned All District on the season. Malcom Selma, a future coach at LHS was also a key player on this team.

Chris Watson   Daryl Joiner   Terrance Blake

In 2006, the Cats had a losing season. No playoff spot was earned. Frank Larry earned All-District honors for the season, making him a 4 year All-District honoree---an award that cannot be eclipsed. In 2007, LHS returned to winning form, finishing the year at 16-12. Playoffs would not be in the cards for the Cats on this year, either. Marcus Rim earned All-District accolades on the season. In 2008, Leesville again dipped below .500 and finished the season 17-18. Dionte Kennedy was named All-District on the season.

Coach Reese resigned his post at LHS after the 2008 season and took the head coaching job at Anacoco. Reese found significant success coaching his alma mater and his squads at AHS won state titles in 2015 and 2016.

Former LHS standout Reggie Degray was hired to coach the Wampus Cats in 2009. The Cats returned to winning form and earned a playoff berth, but lost in the first round of the tournament to Bossier High School. All-State footballer Levander Liggins earned All-District honors for the black and gold in the 2009 season.

Marcus Rim   Dionte Kennedy   Norman Allen   Jeron Hamm

2000's: Lady Cats

Iin the 2000 season, Coach Sowells and his team kept winning. The Lady Wampus Cats won the district and finished the season with a 14-14 record. Sheronda Bowers,and Natasha Johnson were named to the All-District team and Coach Joe Sowells earned Coach of the Year Honor. Leesville made the playoffs, but the Lady Cats were eliminated in the first round. in a game with Bolton.

Shernda Bowers   Natasha Thomas

In 2001, the Lady Cats again won their district and finished the season with a record of 20-13. Sheronda Bowers led the squad in scoring with a 26 points per game average and made All-State for the season. Sheronda, Natasha Johnson and Ebony Parker were All-District selections. Bowers signed with McNeese State to play collegiately and competed for four years for the Cowgirls. The Lady Cats lost in the first round of the playoffs to Pineville.

Girls' First Team

Player	School	Ht.	Class	PPG
Seimone Augustus	Capitol	6-1	Jr.	22.0
Chelsea Newton	Carroll	5-11	Sr.	28.4
Christy Pantallion	Bolton	5-7	Jr.	24.0
Ebony Owens	St. Mary's (N.O.)	5-10	Sr.	19.4
Crystal Smith	Haughton	5-5	Jr.	29.5

Girls' Second Team

Player	School	Ht.	Class	PPG
Sheronda Bowers	Leesville	5-8	Sr.	26.0
Rebecca Montz	Abbeville	5-5	Sr.	24.0
Carla Robinson	Capitol	5-9	Jr.	13.0
Allison Williams	Ellender	6-1	Sr.	16.3
Yakeisha Lewis	Assumption	5-11	Sr.	19.6

Most Valuable Player: Seimone Augustus, Capitol
Coach of the Year: Alvin Stewart, Capitol

Ebony Parker

Girls' First Team

Pos.	Player	School	Class	Ht.	PPG	RPG	APG	SPG
C	Brandy Bradley	W-Marion	Jr.	5-11	9.9	10.0		
G	Cedrina Charles	DeRidder	Sr.	5-7	17.4	4.4	4.2	3.0
G	Sam Ford	Sam Houston	Sr.	5-0	19.1	4.3		
C/F	Tena Matthews	W-Marion	Jr.	5-7	17.4	14.0		
C	Regina McClure	Leesville	Sr.	5-10	13.6	9.8		

Girls' Second Team

Player	School	Class	Ht.	PPG	RPG	APG	SPG
Lois Guillory	W-Marion						
Shonte Kennedy	Leesville						
Keisha Lampkin	W-Marion						
Rebecca Lund	DeRidder	Sr.	5-7	8.0	4.8	2.1	2.0
Erin Smith	Leesville						

Regina McClure

In 2002, Coach Sowell's Lady Wampus Cats kept winning, finishing the season with a record of 17-10. Regina McClure, Shonte Kennedy and Erin Smith earned All-District honors on the years, with McClure also making first team ALL CENLA. In 2003, the squad finished 12-16 on the season. Shonte Kennedy (22 PPG) and Brett Funderburk earned All-District honors. Kennedy was also selected for the All-State team on the season.

Courtney Carter   Shonte Kennedy

In 2004, the Cats returned to winning form, notching a 20-11 season and earning a playoff bid. In the post season, LHS went out in the first round to a tough squad from Dutchtown. Shonte Kennedy, Courtney Carte and Jennifer Blake each earned All-District awards. Kennedy signed with NSU and Funderburk inked a scholarship with ULM.

Bretta Funderburk

In 2005, Coach Sowell's squad had a great year, compiling an overall record of 26-6. The Lady Wampus Cats won their district outright and earned a spot in the state playoffs. In the state tournament, the Cats beat Sam Houston in the first round and fell just short in a game against Broadmoor (Baton Rouge) in the regional round. The 26 win tally was the most for an LHS team since the 1950s. Shonte Kennedy and Courtney Carter earned All-District. Carter was named All-State and signed a scholarhsip offer with the University of Louisiana at Monroe

GIRLS				DISTRICT 3-4A GIRLS		
First Team				**FIRST TEAM**		
Keshonda Carrier, LaGrange	6-5	Sr.	24.1	Courtney Carter, Leesville	Sr.	22.1
Brittany Helm, Glen Oaks	5-8	Jr.	21.0	Shonte Kennedy, Leesville	Sr.	11.9
Tysheka Grimes, Capitol	6-0	Jr.	18.0	Emily Palermo, Pineville	Jr.	15.0
Latashia Wise, Assumption	5-9	Sr.	17.1	Kayla Guidry, Peabody	Jr.	14.0
Whitney Dunlap, Bishop Sullivan	5-7	Sr.	20.1	Kelli Brasher, Peabody	Sr.	12.0
Second Team				**SECOND TEAM**		
LaShonda Smith, Bastrop	5-4	Jr.	16.0	LaShonda Swafford, Tioga	Jr.	11.4
Candice McGee, Cabrini	5-11	Jr.	12.8	Courtney Barber, Tioga	Soph.	9.0
Courtney Carter, Leesville	5-8	Sr.	22.1	Lindsay Lewis, Pineville	Sr.	13.0
Reisha Bullock, De La Salle	5-11	Jr.	21.4	Caitlynn Neely, ASH	Jr.	11.1
Teagra Clifton, Capitol	5-10	So.	15.0	Jennifer Blaker, Leesville	Jr.	8.2
				MOST VALUABLE PLAYER		
				Courtney Carter, Leesville		
				COACH OF THE YEAR		
				Joe Sowell, Leesville		

2006 would be Coach Sowell's last year at the helm for LHS basketball. His squad finished the year with a 10-18 record and Jennifer Blake earned All-District honors. Upon the conclusion of the 2006 season, Joe Sowells was the all-time winningest coach in Leesville High School in terms of total wins. His 213 wins is almost 150 more than second place all time (Louise Bonin). His 7 district titles also stand alone as the most in Wampus Cat girls' basketball history.

Cornelia Miller took the reigns of the Lady Cats' basketball program for two years—2007 and 2008. The records in the two seasons were 11-16 and 4-24, respectively. No athletes earned All-District honors in 2007. Tiffany Wallace and Alyse Lacking earned All-District honors in 2008. In 2009, Robert Carter was named as head coach and the squad went 8-12 on the season. Tiffany Wallace and Chelsea Martin were named All-District for the 2009 season. No playoff spots were earned in 2007, 2008, or 2009.

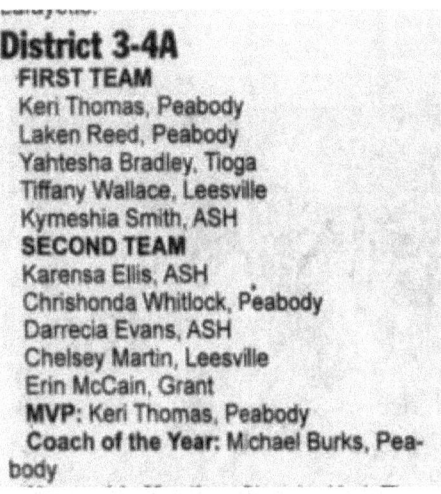

District 3-4A
First Team
Alonda Williams, Peabody, Sr.
Shambrica Chatman, Peabody, Sr.
Karensa Ellis, ASH, Jr.
Shemekia Jones, Grant, Sr.
Aeriona Ray, Tioga, So.
Second Team
Cara Miley, Tioga, Fr.
Tiffany Wallace, Leesville, Fr.
Alyse Lacking, Leesville, Sr.
Chrishonda Whitlock, Peabody, So.
Allison Evans, ASH, Jr.
Hannah Jeffress, Grant, Sr.
Most Valuable Player: Alonda Williams, Peabody
Coach of the Year: Carol Elder, ASH

2008 All-District

District 3-4A
FIRST TEAM
Keri Thomas, Peabody
Laken Reed, Peabody
Yahtesha Bradley, Tioga
Tiffany Wallace, Leesville
Kymeshia Smith, ASH
SECOND TEAM
Karensa Ellis, ASH
Chrishonda Whitlock, Peabody
Darrecia Evans, ASH
Chelsey Martin, Leesville
Erin McCain, Grant
MVP: Keri Thomas, Peabody
Coach of the Year: Michael Burks, Peabody

2009 All-District

2010-2019: Consistent Winning, Back to the Top 28

In the Fall of 2009, Carl Mastrosimone was hired as the head coach for LHS boys' basketball. Coach "Mastro" as he was called, was hired out of Killeen Texas to coach and would spend 7 years on the bench with the Wampus Cats. In his first year (2010), the Cats went 5-15 and did not make the playoffs. Levander Liggins repeated as an All-District performer for the season. Quick word on Liggins: Levander was a multi-sport star at LHS. He earned All-State honors in football and track (Long Jump champion) in addition to being a two-time All-District performer in basketball; he also went on to earn 4 varisty letters in collegiate football at Louisian Tech and was a free agent with the Houston Texans.

In 2011, Leesville got back on the winning track and finished the season with a 17-14 record, earning a playoff spot. The Cats fell to powerhouse Huntington (Shreveport) in the first round of the state playoffs. LaShawn Walters earned All-District honors on the season. In 2012, Leesville went 17-12 on the season and their post season experience was just like 2011, with a first round loss to Huntingon. Darren McQueen earned All-District honors for the season.

Tyshawn Johnson   Roderick Kelly   Coach Mastro

For the 2013 season, the Wampus Cats performed brilliantly, finishing the season with a record of 27-6. Coach Mastro's squad finished second in the district to perennial power Peabody, and earned a 12 seed in the playoffs; Leesvill won a first round game against Hammond but fell in the second round to East Jefferson. Vidall Corbin and Darren McQueen earned All-District honors for the season. Early in the year, McQueen poured in 46 points in a game against Parkway (Bossier City), tieing Gary McDonald's scoring record of 46 set in 1970. In 2014, the Cats kept winning, finishing with a record of 17-14 Corbin repeated as All-District. The Cats went into the playoffs and lost in the first round to Northside.

Vidall Corbin   Darren McQueen   Trevon Hairston   Mastro & Westerchil

In 2015, the Wampus Cat went 27-6 on the year. The black and gold tied for first in the district with Peabody and earned a playoff spot. In the first round of the post season, the Cats beat Cecilia on the road. In the second round St. Michael (formerly Bishop Sullivan) of Baton Rouge ended the Cat's season. DaShawn Lewis (Dist MVP, 13PPG, 8 Reb), Darrion Jaiswal and Derrick Brock were All-District honorees. Joining Coach Mastro on the bench as an assistant was former head coach Grant Westerchil, whose son Brady was a key player on the squad for several years in high school.

Derrick Brock   DaShawn Lewis   Darrion Jaiswal & Brady Westerchil

In 2016, Coach Mastro's squad finished the year with a 21-14 record. Though not a district champion, the Cats still earned a spot in the state playoffs. Leesville traveled to Carencro for the tournament game but was eliminated. On the year, Derrick Brock and Darion Nabors were named All-District.

2017 would be Mastro's final year at the helm of the black and gold. His squad finished 11-21 and did manage a playoff appearance. Terrell Lucas was named to the All District team. Mastrosimone put up a career win total of 139-108, a .56 winning percentage. Under Mastro, the Cats were always competitive, were consistent winners and earned 7 post-season appearances, a district title and two post-season wins.

In 2018, Tony Grigg was hired to coach the black and gold. In Grigg's first year, LHS went 20-12 on the season and earned a playoff spot. Opelousas knocked Leesville out in the first round. Dual-sport star Duwon Tolbert was named first team All-District.

In 2019, LHS made a dash to the state's final 4. Grigg's squad put up 33 wins and only four losses on the season. In district play, the Wampus Cats ran the table and earned a #2 seed in the State tournament. In the playoffs, Leesville defeated Tara, Northside and Plaquemine enroute to a berth in the Top 28 (Final 4). Leesville fell to Breaux Bridge on Fat Tuesday in Lake Charles in the semi-finals, but the year was one for the record books. Duwon Tolbert (Dist MPV, and All CENLA), Seginald Bryant, Carlos Sepulveda, Deandre Wilson and Camile Canon all earned All-District honors on the year. Tolbert would be named first team All-State and signed collegiately to play football at Tyler Junior College. He also won the State High Jump competition at the Track and Field championships in May. Bryant signed to play at the next level with LSU-Alexandria.

Duwon Tolbert

Final Score, Quarterfinals at home   Seginald Bryant

Deandre Wilson

LHS Lady Wampus Cats 2010-2019

The 2010 and 2011 years were very similar and should be discussed in the same context. Robert Carter, a former LHS player who had spent a full career in law enforcement had come to Leesville high a few years previously and was hired in 2009 to lead the team. Carter molded a talented group of athletes into a competitive team.

In 2010, the Lady Cats went 18-14 on the year and earned a playoff berth. Leesville traveled to St. Louis for the playoff game but the girls were defeated by the Saints. Key players for the team were Tiffany Wallace and Chelsea Martin and both earned All-District honors. Wallace averaged 29.0 points per game on the season---the highest discovered for a Lady Wampus Cat in the research for this book. Tiffany also earned All-State honors and established herself as a prolific scorer.

In 2011, Carter's squad went 20-7 on the season. The black and gold just missed a district title, falling short to Peabody of Alexandria. In the post season, Leesville defeated Ellender in the first round, but fell to Helen Cox on the road in a tough loss amidst questionable officiating. Wallace and Martin were named All District, as was Freshman Malachi McQueen. Martin earned All-State honors in her senior campaign. It should be noted that Chelsea Manning left LHS as a 3 time All-District performer and Tiffany Wallace notched the same award for FOUR consecutive years, tying Frank Larry as a 4 time All-District performer. After her senior year, Wallace signed a National Letter of Intent to play for the University of New Orleans.

Chelsea Martin
All-State 2011

Tiffany Wallace
All-State 2010

Robert Carter

In 2012, Amanda Clemons would be hired to Coach the Lady Wampus Cats. In her first year, the Lady Cats went 9-14 on the season. No post-season spot was earned in the season. Malachi McQueen and Linda Rogers earned All-District honors.

In 2013, Coach Clemons' team had a big year---going 24-8 on the season and almost winning a district title. In the post season, the Lady Cats picked up a first round win at Bellaire (Baton Rouge), but were put out of the playoffs in the regional round by Neville. All District were Bralie Fields (Dist MVP); Malachi McQueen and Linda Rogers. Malachi McQueen signed to play collegiately with Angelina Jr. College (Texas).

Malachi McQueen   Bralie Fields

The 2014 season saw the Lady Wampus Cats go 3-15 on the year. No playoffs were earned and no athletes were named All-District.

In 2015, Eric Guidry was hired to coach the black and gold and he got the team on the winning track, going 16-8 on the year. The squad earned a playoff spot, but had to face a tough Loyola team that dispatched the Lady Cats in the first round. All District performers for the year were Keshera Culbert (17.3 PPG) and Linda Rogers. Guidry left LHS after one year and Summer Sexson-Peters was hired as head coach. In 2016 and 2017, the Lady Cats compiled records of 7-18 and 9-18. After the 2017 season, the Cats did earn a post-season spot, but were put out by Huntington in the first round. Keke Culbert and J'mani Ingram were all district performers.

KeKe Culbert

Delicia Rushing & Gabriella Gray

The Lady Cats hired a new coach for the 2018-2019 season. Kristi Perkins, an experienced signal caller from Jena led the Lady Wampus Cats to back to back playoff appearances during her time as head coach. In 2018, the team went 19-14 and earned a playoff spot. In the post-season, Leesville won one game (vs Woodlawn of Shreveport) and lost one (Neville of Monroe). On the year, 3 Wampus Cats earned All-District honors: Kerrigan Small (18.2 PPG), Jakayla Collins, and Dadriana Ford. Kerrigan Small also earned All-State honors and played collegiately with Apprentice School Builders.

In 2019, the Lady Cats fell below the .500 mark but still managed a playoff berth. The squad fell to Assumption. JaRielle James and Dadrienne Ford earned All-District honors on the season.

Kerrigan Small
All-State 2018

ZaKayla Collins

2020 and Beyond

When the COVID pandemic was declared in 2020 and the world was shutdown, including schools, the Wampus Cats had just finished a losing season. One year coach Josh Timberlake had guided the Cats to a 13-18 season with no post-season appearance. Carolos Pagan was named All-District for the season.

For the ensuing three years, the Cats really struggled. The records for 2021, 2022 and 2023 were 6-16, 7-16 and 8-21. No LHS player was named to the All-District squad for this three year period and no playoff spots were earned.

Carlos Pagan   Ju'liun Culbert

In 2024, LHS hired Jordan Andrews as head coach. The son of a coach and successful high school player and coach, Andrews went about putting LHS back on a winning track. For the season, the Wampus Cats went 13-17 and earned Wildcard spot in the playoffs. Leesville went on the road and lost a tough, first round contest to Minden. Football standout Jeremiah Lee earned All-District honors on the season and All-State running back Xavier Ford came out for basketball and led the district in rebounds.

2020-2024 Lady Cats

2020 and 2021 were very tough years for the Lady Wampus Cats. In 2020, the squad went 2-27 and Jayla Burnett was named All-District. In 2021, the final record was 2-16. No playoffs were achieved in either season

In 2022, Brandon Jordan was hired and he got the Lady Cats back in the post season and played just below .500 basketball with a 12-13 season.

2023 and 2024 seasons were very solid seasons for the Lady Wampus Cats. In both years, the squad played well above .500 and both teams made it to the playoffs and won their first round games in the playoffs; a search of records indicates that back-to-back seasons with a playoff win hadn't happened in 70 years. Coach Caitlyn Gentry (now Sciabarassi) was hired in 2023 and she returned in 2024. Joining Coach Sciabarassi on the sideline as assistant was former LHS standout Cornelia Miller. Jade LeDay, Shyann McCummings and Tekeirah Harris all were selected as All-District in 2023 and Coach Gentry was named 2023's Coach of the Year. In 2024, Shyann McCummings (Dist MVP/24.8 PPG) and Tekeirah Harris were named to the All-District teams again. McCummings passed the 1,000 point milestone midway through her junior year and at this writing, is scheduled to come back for her senior campaign.

Shyann McCummings   Tekeriah Harris   Kadence Reibold

Piper Fowler   Jakiyra Wilson   2023-2024 Lady Wampus Cats

The Future: To Be Determined

One thing is for certain: Basketball is important to Leesville High School. As these pages have illustrated, LHS has had some great players and great teams.   We've had good years, lean years, and some occasional great years. The future is as bright as the players and the community want to make it.   The ensuing pages will provide additional pictures and some info on coach records and season-by-season snapshots.

Coaches at Leesville High School---Boys and Girls

The Wampus Cat boys' and girls' teams have had a number of coaches through the decades. Since the early 1950s. 17 boys' coaches and 24 girls' coaches can be identified.

For boys' coaches, the average time in the position of head coach is 4.2 years. For girl's coaches, the head signal caller's average tenure is just over two years.

On the boy's side: Hub Jordan and Bill Bennett account for the most wins in LHS history. Both men coached the Wampus Cats for 11 years. Jordan eclipsed Bennett in his final year and tallied 239 wins, whereas Bennett finished his career with 232. Grant Westerchil is third all-time in wins with 179, and Carl Mastro is fourth, with 136. In terms of winning percentages, Westerchil is the all-time leader with a .76 win percent. Tony Grigg, a two year head coach is second all time. Jordan is third in win percentages and Michael Mallet is fourth.

Westerchil is first all time with 6 district titles, and he is tied with Carl Mastro in terms of total playoff appearances in a career. Westerchil took his team to the state playoffs every year as a head coach and led the Cats to the state title in 2001.

On the girls' side, Joe Sowells is the unquestioned leader in terms of wins with 213. Second and third all time with wins were Louise Bonin (88) and Guinell Smart (81). Sowells is also the leader in district titles with 7 and playoff appearances (10). In terms of winning percentages, Guinnell Smart is far and away the statistical leader. Coach Smart compiled a record 81-4 in her brief period of coaching in the 1950s. Second all time is AL Temple, a two-year coach in the 50s. Smart and Temple also led the girls' team to the state runner up spots in 1951 and 54, respectively.

Two coaches, Michael Mallet and Bill Bennett coached boys' and girls' team—at the same time. Interestingly, both years were good years for the Lady Cats and Cats.

Grant Westerchil, Richard Reese and Reggie DeGray were former LHS players who returned to the bench to coach the boys' teams. Michael Mallet was not a LHS player---but played ball in Leesville at Vernon High School (closed in 1969). On the girls' side, Cornelia Miller and Summer Sexton Peters were former players who came back to coach at their alma mater

Boys' Coaches: Total Wins

Coach	Wins	Losses	Tenure	Winning %	Dist Champs	Playoff Appearances
Hub Jordan	239	104	1984-94	0.69	3	6
Bill Bennett	232	155	1953-63	0.59	2	4
Grant Westerchil	179	55	1995-2001	0.76	6	7
Carl Mastro	136	92	2010-2017	0.59	1	7
Tracy Reese	128	86	2002-2008	0.59	1	4
Michael Mallet	125	70	1977-1983	0.64	2	4
Keith Andrews	87	54	1973-1976	0.61	1	2
Richard Reese	42	44	1970-1972	0.49	1	1
Tony Grigg	42	16	2018-2019	0.72	1	1
Bobby Craft	32	34	1967-1968	0.49	0	0
Jimmy Leach	22	12	1969	0.64	0	0
Reggie DeGray	17	16	2019	0.51	0	1
Ralph Kees	15	11	1965	0.57	0	0
Jordan Andrews	13	16	2024	0.44	0	1
Richie Dixon	13	31	2021-2022	0.29	0	0
Josh Timberlake	13	18	2020	0.41	0	0
Ed Young	8	10	1966	0.44	0	0

Hub Jordan   Billy Bennett   Carl Mastro

Boys' Coaches, Winning Percentage

Coach	Winning %	Wins	Losses	Tenure
Grant Westerchil	0.76	179	55	1995-2001
Tony Grigg	0.72	42	16	2018-2019
Hub Jordan	0.69	239	104	1984-94
Michael Mallet	0.64	125	70	1977-1983
Jimmy Leach	0.64	22	12	1969
Keith Andrews	0.61	87	54	1973-1976
Bill Bennett	0.59	232	155	1953-63
Carl Mastro	0.59	136	92	2010-2017
Tracy Reese	0.59	128	86	2002-2008
Ralph Kees	0.57	15	1	1965
Reggie DeGray	0.51	17	16	2019
Richard Reese	0.49	42	44	1970-1972
Bobby Craft	0.49	32	34	1967-1968
Jordan Andrews	0.44	13	16	2024
Ed Young	0.44	8	10	1966
Josh Timberlake	0.41	13	18	2020
Richie Dixon	0.29	13	31	2021-2022

Grant Westerchil

Michael Mallet

Keith Andrews

Richard Reese

Girls' Coaches: Total Wins

Coach	Wins	Losses	Tenure	Winning %	Dist Champs	Playoff Appearances
Joe Sowells	213	136	1995-2006	0.61	7	10
Louise Bonin	88	65	1988-1992	0.57	2	4
Guinell Smart	81	4	1952-1954	0.95	3	3
AL Temple	63	14	1950-1951	0.81	1	2
Amanda Clemons	52	44	2012-2015	0.54	0	1
Robert Carter	46	33	2009-2011	0.58	0	2
Caitlyn Sciabarassi	38	20	2023-pres	0.65	0	2
Angela Self	29	35	1985-1987	0.45	0	0
Krista Perkins	31	32	2018-2019	0.47	0	2
Billy Crawford	17	29	1976-1977	0.36	0	0
Summer Sexson	16	36	2016-2017	0.3	0	1
Eric Guidry	16	8	2015	0.67	0	1
Mike Mallet	16	7	1982	69	0	0
Cornelia Miller	15	40	2007-2008	0.27	0	0
Bill Benett	13	7	1956	0.65	1	1
Kay Taylor	10	12	1984	0.45	0	0
Agatha Rhodes	10	14	1960	0.41	0	0
Jacob Anderson	9	17	1955	0.34	0	0
Kay Stephens	8	12	1980-1981	0.4	0	0
Brandon Jordan	3	10	2021	0.23	0	0
Hub Jordan	3	18	1983	0.14	0	0
Janet Manuel	3	37	1978-1979	0.07	0	0
Lara Cooley	2	13	2020	0.13	0	0
Daniel Greenhouse	2	27	2020	0.06	0	0

Guinnell Smart　　　　Joe Sowells　　　　Billy Crawford

Girls' Coaches, Winning Percentage

Coach	Winning%	Wins	Losses	Tenure
Guinell Smart	0.95	81	4	1952-1954
AL Temple*	0.81	63	14	1950-1951
Mike Mallet	0.69	16	7	1982
Eric Guidry	0.67	16	8	2015
Caitlyn Sciabarassi	0.65	38	20	2023-pres
Bill Benett	0.65	13	7	1956
Joe Sowells	0.61	213	136	1995-2006
Robert Carter	0.58	46	33	2009-2011
Louise Bonin	0.57	88	65	1988-1992
Amanda Clemons	0.54	52	44	2012-2015
Krista Perkins	0.47	31	32	2018-2019
Angela Self	0.45	29	35	1985-1987
Kay Taylor	0.45	10	12	1984
Agatha Rhodes	0.41	10	14	1960
Kay Stephens	0.4	8	12	1980-1981
Billy Crawford	0.36	17	29	1976-1977
Jacob Anderson	0.34	9	17	1955
Summer Sexson	0.3	16	36	2016-2017
Cornelia Miller	0.27	15	40	2007-2008
Brandon Jordan	0.23	3	10	2021
Hub Jordan	0.14	3	18	1983
Lara Cooley	0.13	2	13	2020
Janet Manuel	0.07	3	37	1978-1979
Daniel Greenhouse	0.06	2	27	2020

Caitlyn Sciarbarassi   Amanda Clemons   Kristi Perkins   Louise Bonin

Year-by-Year, LHS Win/Loss Records, Playoff Appearances, District Titles, Head Coaches, Notes and All-District and All-State Performers

School Year	Wins	Losses	Playoffs	Dist Champ	Head Coach	Notes	All Dist/All State
2024	13	16	Y	N	Jordan Andrews		Jeremiah Lee
2023	8	21	N	N	Richie Dixon		Julian Colbert
2022	7	15	N	N	Rickie Dixon		
2021	6	16	N	N	Rickie Dixon		
2020	13	18	N	N	Josh Timberlake		Carlos Pagan
2019	32	4	Y	Y	Tony Grigg	State Semi Finals; beat Tara, Northside and Plaquemine; lost to Breaux Bridge in semifinals. Undefeated in Dist.	Duwon Tolbert (Dist MVP, All CENLA and ALL STATE); Seginald Bryant; Carlos Sepulveda; Deandre Wilson; Camile Canon
2018	20	12	Y	N	Tony Grigg	Lost in 1st round to Opelousas	Duwon Tolbert
2017	11	21	Y	N	Carl Mastrosimone	Lost in 1st round to Washington-Marion	Terrell Lucas
2016	21	14	Y	N	Carl Mastrosimone	Lost in 1st round to Carencro	Derrick Brock, Darion Nabors
2015	24	8	Y	Y (tie)	Carl Mastrosimone	Lost to St. Michael in 2nd Round; beat Cecilia in 1st round	DaShawn Lewis (Dist MVP, 13PPG, 8 Reb); Darrion Jaiswal; Derrick Brock
2014	17	14	Y	N	Carl Mastrosimone	Lost in 1st round to Northside	Vidall Corbin

School Year	Wins	Losses	Playoffs	Dist Champ	Head Coach	Notes	All Dist/All State
2013	27	6	Y	N	Carl Mastrosimone	Lost in 2nd round to East Jefferson; beat Hammon in 1st round. Darren McQueen scored 46 pts in a game vs Parkway, tying Gary McDonald's record from 1970	Vidall Corbin; Darren McQueen

School Year	Wins	Losses	Playoffs	Dist Champ	Head Coach	Notes	All Dist/All State
2012	17	12	Y	N	Carl Mastrosimone	Lost in 1st round to Huntington	Darren McQueen
2011	17	14	Y	N	Carl Mastrosimone	Lost in 1st round to Huntington	LaShawn Waters (15.7 PPG)
2010	5	19	N	N	Carl Mastrosimone		Levander Liggins
2009	17	16	Y	N	Reggie Degray	Lost to Bossier in 1st round	Levander Liggins
2008	17	18	N	N	Tracy Reese		Dionte Kennedy
2007	16	12	N	N	Tracy Reese		Marcus Rim
2006	12	14	N	N	Tracy Reese		Frank Larry
2005	27	8	Y	Y (tie)	Tracy Reese	Lost 1st round to Opelousas	Frank Larry, Terrance Blake; Daryl Joiner All Dist, All CENLA
2004	23	11	y	N	Tracy Reese	Lost in 1st round to Istrouma	Terrance Blake; Frank Larry
2003	19	11	Y	N	Tracy Reese	Lost in 1st round in Hannan	Daryl Joiner, Frank Larry
2002	20	10	Y	N	Tracy Reese	Lost in 2nd round to St. Martinville; beat Bastrop in 1st round	Marcus Johnson, Eric Woods (17.9 PPG). Eric Woods All-State

School Year	Wins	Losses	Playoffs	Dist Champ	Head Coach	Notes	All Dist/All State
2001	28	8	y	y	Grant Westerchil	State Champions; defeated Woodlawn in title game. Defeated Scotlandville in 1st round; defeated St Thomas Moore in quarterfinals; defeated Carver in semi-finals. Woods signs with LA Tech	Eric Woods (21.8 PPG); Chris Campbell; Marcus Johnson. Eric Woods All-State
2000	33	5	y	y	Grant Westerchil	State Runner up; lost to Peabody in finals; defeated Salmen in semi-finals; defeated Parkway in quarters; defeated Lee in 2nd round	Darnell Bradley (19.8 PPG); Eric Woods; Chris Campbell. Darnell Bradley All-State. Coach Westerchil Coach of the Year
1999	24	7	Y	N	Grant Westerchil	Defeated Bishop Sullivan 1st round; lost to Baker in 2nd round	Derek Wright (23.5 PPG); Darnell Bradley. Derek Wright All-State.
1998	21	8	Y	Y (tie)	Grant Westerchil	Lost to Hammond in 2nd round	JJ Joiner (Dist MVP/19.5 PPG); Jeff Brown; Derek Wright. JJ Joiner All-State.
1997	25	9	Y	Y	Grant Westerchil	defeated Haughton in the 1st round; lost to Cohen in round 2	JJ Joiner; Jamal Wilson

School Year	Wins	Losses	Playoffs	Dist Champ	Head Coach	Notes	All Dist/All State
1996	27	8	Y	Y	Grant Westerchil	State Runner up; lost to Cohen in finals; Defeated St. Thomas More (semi), Carroll (quarter); Tioga in 2nd round; Undefeated in district play. Reggie DeGray signed with Wofford	Demond Mallet (MVP, 27.6 PPG); Reggie DeGray; Lonnie Thomas; Coach Westerchil Dist Coach of the Year. Demond Mallet and Reggie Degray All-State.
1995	21	10	Y	Y	Grant Westerchil	Lost in 1st round to Pineville; undefeated in district	Demond Mallet (22 MPG); Reggie DeGray; Lonnie Thomas; Demond Mallet All-State; Westerchil Coach of the Year
1994	25	8	Y	Y (tie)	Hub Jordan	Won 1st round vs Wossman; lost to Glen Oaks in 2nd round. Ronnie DeGray signed with Colorado	Ronnie DeGray (17 PPG); Montrel Dorsey
1993	20	10	N	N	Hub Jordan	tied for 2nd in district; went into a playoff to get into playoffs vs LaGrange and lost	Ennis Flowers
1992	21	11	Y	N	Hub Jordan	Lost in 1st round to Huntington; Dist runner up	Ennis Flowers (16 PPG); Ray Falero; Kavika Pittman

School Year	Wins	Losses	Playoffs	Dist Champ	Head Coach	Notes	All Dist/All State
1991	25	10	Y	Y	Hub Jordan	Defeated Northside in 1st round; lost in 2nd round to Capitol	Patrick Kennedy (MVP, 25.2 PPG); Ennis Flowers; Scott Larue
1990	27	7	Y	N	Hub Jordan	1st round loss to New Iberia	Miguel Yepez
1989	29	4	Y	Y	Hub Jordan	State Semi-Finals. Defeated New Iberia in 1st round, Robert. E. Lee in 2nd round; Captain Shreve in quarterfinals; lost so Shaw in Semi-Finals	Robert Salisbury (17.8 PPG); Eric Rhodes; Neal Travis;
1988	12	16	N	N	Hub Jordan		Robert Salisbury
1987	20	7	N	N	Hub Jordan		Michael Joiner (25 PPG); Anthony Burns. Michael Joiner All-State
1986	16	13	N	N	Hub Jordan	Marro Hawkins signs with Centenary	Michael Joiner; Anthony Burns
1985	29	6	Y	N	Hub Jordan	State Semi-finalist, lost to Amite; defeated ASH in quarters; defeated St. Thomas More in 2nd round; Port Allen in 1st round	Tony Marsh (18.1 PPG); Darrell Jones
1984	17	12	N	N	Hub Jordan	7-5 in district	Grant Westerchil. Randy Kennedy
1983	30	4	Y	Y	Michael Mallet	defeated Rayne in 1st round; lost to Richwood in Quarterfinals	Nikita Wilson (18.5 PPG); Steve Travis; Steve Kennedy; Grant Westerchil. Nikita Wilson All-State & All-American

School Year	Wins	Losses	Playoffs	Dist Champ	Head Coach	Notes	All Dist/All State
1982	25	1	Y	Y	Michael Mallet	Lost 1st round game to Crowley	Nikita Wilson; Shelton Hickerson; Eric Travis; Michael Mallet Coach of the Year
1981	16	11	N	N	Michael Mallet		Levon White
1979	9	17	N	N	Michael Mallet		
1978	21	10	Y	N	Michael Mallet	Lost to Peabody in 1st round	Cedric Johnson; Jerry Lynch
1977	21	12	Y	N	Michael Mallet	Tied for 2nd with Jennings in district, won a play-in game. Lost to Pineville in regional round	Cedric Johnson; Jerry Lynch
1976	16	19	N	N	Keith Andrews		Cedric Johnson
1975	30	7	Y	Y	Keith Andrews	Undefeated District Champs (10-0); lost in 1st round to Peabody.	John Joiner (MVP); Deano Brown; Randall Smith; Coach Andrews Coach of the Year

School Year	Wins	Losses	Playoffs	Dist Champ	Head Coach	Notes	All Dist/All State
1974	24	13	N	N	Keith Andrews	3rd place in district	John Joiner; Robert Walker
1973	20	15	Y	N	Keith Andrews	tied for 2nd in district with Oakdale; lost a play-in game for a spot in state tournament	Floyd Tinsley
1972	6	22	N	N	Richard Reese		
1971	15	16	N	N	Richard Reese		

School Year	Wins	Losses	Playoffs	Dist Champ	Head Coach	Notes	All Dist/All State
1970	23	11	Y	Y (tie)	Richard Reese	Lost to DeRidder in 1st round of tournament. Robert Blow is 1st team All-District in 1st season after school merger; Gary McDonald scored 46 points, school record to this point	Robert Blow; Gary McDonald; Steve Laurence
1969	22	10	N	N	Jimmy Leach		Asa Skinner; Gary McDonald; Steve Laurence
1968	15	17	N	N	Bobby Craft		
1967	17	17	N	N	Bobby Craft		Tim Lynch
1966	8	10	N	N	Ed Young		John Henson; Joe Gendron; James Latham
1965	15	11	N	N	Ralph Kees	Tied for 2nd; lost play-in for playoff spot with Menard	Junior Temple
1964	16	8	N	N	Billy Bennett (last year)	Richard Schwarts State scoring leader--29.3 PPG	Richard Schwartz; Billy Crawford. Richard Schwartz All-State
1963	2	24	N	N	Billy Bennett		Edwin Cabra; Richard Schwartz

School Year	Wins	Losses	Playoffs	Dist Champ	Head Coach	Notes	All Dist/All State
1962	10	18	N	N	Billy Bennett		Danny Hardwick; Bobby Craft

Year	W	L	?	?	Coach	Notes	Honors
1961	28	7	N	N	Billy Bennett	No playoffs: Richard Reese sets school single-season (901) and career (2005) record for scoring. 42 was single game high. Avg 23.6 per game.	Richard Reese: All-Dist, All-State and State Player of the Year
1960	19	16	N	N	Billy Bennett		
1959	20	14	N	N	Billy Bennett	Hardwick 22.3 PPG. Hardwick scored 40 points in a single game---a record at the time.	Dale Hardwick All-Dist and All-State
1958	24	10	Y	N	Billy Bennett	Won 1st round vs Oakdale; lost to	Dale Hardwick; Lewis Massey; JC Welch.
1957	10	10			Billy Bennett	Not much data can be found; news reports only	
1956	20	13	N	N	Billy Bennett		
1955	28	11	Y	N	Billy Bennett	Lost to Port Barre in 1st round of state tournament	Jimmy Edwards (scoring leader) and Don Goins
1954	28	14	Y	Y	Billy Bennett	Won district tournament; lost in 1st round of state tournament	Larry Goins; Eugene Ammons; Eber Sandell
1953	27	10	Y	Y	Billy Bennett	3rd in District Tournament; lost in 1st round of state tournament to Jonesboro	Elber Sandell All-State

School Year	Wins	Losses	Playoffs	Dist Champ	Head Coach	Notes	All Dist/All State
1952	2	10			Zolon Stiles		
1951			Y	N	Zolon Stiles	Lost 1st round to Cathedral in State Tournament	
1950	18	5			Zolon Stiles		
1948	3	6			Edlo Bray		
1947	1	3			Edlo Bray		
1931	15	1			"Red" Beeson	State Runner-Up; lost to Dry Creek in State Finals	Johnny Pelt All-State
TOTALS	1424	887					

Girls' Basketball Year-by-Year

School Year	Wins	Losses	Playoffs	Dist Champ	Head Coach	Notes	All Dist/All State
2024	21	11	Y	N	Caitlyn (Gentry) Sciabarassi	Won 1st round vs Minden; lost 2nd round to South Beauregard	Shyann McCummings (Dist MVP/24.8 PPG); Tekeirah Harris
2023	18	12	Y	N	Caitlyn Gentry	Won 1st round at Breaux Bridge; Lost 2nd round at LaGrange	Jade LeDay; Shyann McCummings; Tekeirah Harris; Coach Gentry Coach of the Year
2022	12	13	Y	N	Brandon Jordan	Lost in 1st round to Edna Carr	
2021	2	16	N	N	Lara Cooley		
2020	2	27	N	N	Daniel Greenhouse		Jayla Burnett
2019	12	18	Y	N	Kristi Perkins	Lost in 1st round to Assumption	JaRielle James, Dadrienne Ford
2018	19	14	Y	N	Kristi Perkins	Won 1st round game vs Woodlawn; Lost in 2nd round to Neville	Kerrigan Small; Jakayla Collins; Dadriana Ford; Kerrigan Small, All-State
2017	9	18	Y	N	Summer	Lost in 1st round to	J'mani Ingram
2016	7	18	N	N	Summer		Keke Culbert
2015	16	8	Y	N	Eric Guidry	Lost 1st round to Loyola	Keshera Culbert; Linda Rogers
2014	3	15	N	N	Amanda Clemons		
2013	24	8	Y	N	Amanda Clemons	Won 1st round vs Belaire; lost in 2nd round to Neville	Bralie Fields (Dist MVP); Malachi McQueen, Linda Rogers. McQueen signs with Angelina Jr. College
2012	9	14	N	N	Amanda Clemons		Malachi McQueen; Linda Rogers
2011	20	7	Y	N	Robert Carter	Won 1st round vs Ellender; lost 2nd round to Helen Cox	Tiffany Wallace; Chelsea Martin; Malachi McQueen. Wallace signs with UNO. Chelsea Martin All-State
2010	18	14	Y	N	Robert Carter	Lost in 1st round to St. Louis	Tiffany Wallace (MVP/29.0 PPG); Chelsea
2009	8	12	N	N	Robert Carter		Tiffany Wallace; Chelsea Martin

School Year	Wins	Losses	Playoffs	Dist Champ	Head Coach	Notes	All Dist/All State
2008	4	24	N	N	Cornelia Miller		Tiffany Wallace, Alyse Lacking

School Year	Wins	Losses	Playoffs	Dist Champ	Head Coach	Notes	All Dist/All State
2007	11	16	N	N	Cornelia Miller		None selected
2006	10	15	N	N	Joe Sowells		Jennifer Blake
2005	26	6	Y	Y	Joe Sowells	Won 1st round vs Sam Houston; lost in 2nd round to Broadmoor	Courtney Carter, All Dist and All CENLA, signed with ULM
2004	20	11	Y	N	Joe Sowells	Lost to Dutchtown 1st round	Shonte Kennedy; Courtney Carter; Jennifer Blake; Kennedy, Carter sign with NSU; Funderburk signs with ULM; Shonte All-State
2003	12	16	Y	N	Joe Sowells	Lost to St. Thomas More 1st round	Shonte Kennedy (22 PPG); Brett Funderburk; Shonte Kennedy All-State
2002	17	10	N	N	Joe Sowells		Regina McClure, Shonte Kennedy, Erin Smith. McClure also 1st team ALL CENLA
2001	20	13	Y	Y	Joe Sowells	Lost in 1st round to Pineville	Sheronda Bowers (26 PPG); Ebony Parker; Sheronda Bowers All-State, signs with McNeese
2000	14	14	Y	N	Joe Sowells	Lost in 1st round to Bolton	Sheronda Bowers (26 PPG); Natasha Johnson
1999	22	7	Y	Y	Joe Sowells	Lost to Bastrop in 1st round	Sheronda Bowers; Viola Thomas; Sepi Toga; Coach Sowells Coach of the Year

School Year	Wins	Losses	Playoffs	Dist Champ	Head Coach	Notes	All Dist/All State
1998	17	11	Y	Y	Joe Sowells	Defeated BTW (Shreve) 1st round; lost to St. Thomas More 2nd round	Angela Davidson; Viola Thomas; Davidson Dist MVP (22 PPG); Angela Davidson All-State, signs with Mississippi State
1997	19	9	Y	Y	Joe Sowells	Lost to Marksville in 1st round	Angela Davidson; Viola Thomas; Coach Sowell Coach of the Year
1996	17	12	Y	Y	Joe Sowells	Lost in 1st round	Angela Davidson (14 PPG); Kurtina Holland
1995	20	12	Y	Y	Joe Sowells	Lost to Opelousas in 2nd Round; defeated Glen Oaks in 1st Round	Tori Daniels; Cornelia Miller; Nikki Hiers. Coach Sowells Coach of the Year
1994	13	15	N	N	Sherry Broocks		Mary McChrystal (11 PPG); Tori Daniel
1993	20	12	Y	N	Louise Bonin	Defeated W. Monroe 1st round; lost to Byrd in 2nd round (5A Season)	Tiffany Clifton: Tracey Thomas Both athletes signed with Tulane
1992	20	8	Y	(3 way ti	Louise Bonin	Lady Cats lost play-in vs Sulphur (5A); lost to Comeaux in 1st round. Thomas and Clifton signed with Tulane.	Tiffany Clifton; Tracey Thomas.
1991	25	7	Y	Y	Louise Bonin	Advanced to quarterfinals. Defeated East Ascension in 2nd round; 1st round bye	Tangie Riley; Carissa Badger; Tiffany Clifton; Coach Bonin Dist Coach of the Year
1990	10	18	N	N	Louise Bonin		Tangie Riley
1989	18	10	Y	N	Louise Bonin	Defeated Ruston in 1st round; lost to Natchitoches in 2nd round	Angie Thomas (MVP/13.8 PPG); Karen Howard
1988	17	10	N	N	Louise Bonin		Melissa Cleary
1987	15	15	N	N	Angela Self		Ginny Freshley
1986	6	15	N	N	Angela Self		

1985	9	5	N	N	Angela Self	Winning record achieved; 9-5 in district;	
1984	12	10	N	N	Kay Taylor		Connie Howard
1983	3	18	N	N	Hub Jordan		
1982	16	7	N	N	Mike Mallet		Monica Boerner (17 PPG); Regina Dixon
1981	8	12	N	N	Kay		Regina Dixon (17.0 PPG)
1980					Kay	Limited/no data	
1979	3	17	N	N	Janet		
1978	0	20	N	N	Janet		

School Year	Wins	Losses	Playoffs	Dist Champ	Head Coach	Notes	All Dist/All State
1977	6	16	N	N	Billy		
1976	11	13	N	N	Billy		Nita Paris
1962						BASKETBALL CANCELLED	
1961					Vernia Gotreaux	Won Leesville Tournament; Colleen Young and Dorothy Davis key players.	
1960	10	14			Agatha Rhodes		
1959					Agatha Rhodes		
1958					Agatha Rhodes	Lost to Tioga in playoffs	
1957	15	6	Y	Y	Bill Bennett	Semifinalist team. Won 1st round game vs. Oakdale; unknown 2nd round; lost to Lake	
1956	13	6	N	N	Bill Bennett		
1955	9	16	N	N	Jacob Anderson		
1954	29	1	Y	Y	Guinell Smart	State Runner up; lost to Winnsboro in finals.	All State: Shirley Cavanaugh; Faye Jeane
1953	36	1	Y	Y	Guinnell Smart	State Semi-Finalist (3rd Place); Defeated Amite in Consolation game; lost to Winnsboro in Semi Final; Defeated Winnfield in quarterfinals	All State: Faye Jeane; Gwendolyn Whittaker; Audrey Chamberlain
1952	16	3	Y		Guinnell Smart	State Semi-Finalist (3rd Place); Defeated Winnfield in Consolation game; lost to Oak Grove in Semi Final; Defeated Scott & St. Joseph in 1st 2 rounds	
School Year	Wins	Losses	Playoffs	Dist Champ	Head Coach	Notes	All Dist/All State

Year							
1951	42	7	Y	Y	A. L. Temple	State Runner Up; Bye in 1st round; def Farmerville in 2nd round; def Many in Quarters; defeated Scott in Semi Finals	All State: Betty Paddy, Jane Carey
1950	21	7			A. L. Temple		
1948	2	6					
1947	1	1					
1913	1	3				1st year of LHS Basketball; players were McDaniel, Averie, McAlpin, Davis, Cudd,	
	836	700					

The Championship Season: 2001

The Wampus Cat Boys' Basketball Team stands alone as the most highly accomplished basketball team in LHS history and one of only 3 teams in LHS history to win a state championship. Coach Grant Westerchil's team went 28-8 on the year and ran the table in the Louisiana High School Athletics Association (LHSAA) state tournament. The Cats won the district in 2001, going 10-0 in league play. In the playoffs, Leesville defeated Scotlandville, St. Thomas Moore, Carver and Woodlawn of Baton Rouge in the title game.

Team members from the 2001 team were Samuel Burley, Ontario Agnew, Gabriel Wilson, Walter Mason, Johnnie Hearns, Jonathan Hopkins, Chris Elkins, Dennis Joiner, David Kelly, Marcus Johnson, Chris Campbell, James Carter, Eric Woods, Aaron Moore, Damien Jones, and manager Logan Morris. Head Coach Westerchil was joined on the bench by Assistant Coach Tracy Reese.

The ensuing pages of chapter consist of items from the Westerchil family scrapbook on the season. Articles and photos compliments of Mrs. Best Westerchil.

Leesville 75, Crowley 69
CROWLEY (11-16, 1-4)
Courtney Allen 4-10 4-4 13, Kevin Perkins 5-17 1-6 11, Chris Charles 3-3 1-1 7, Zach Morgan 2-5 0-0 4, Bryce DeJean 8-15 0-0 16, Steven Moore 2-3 0-2 5, Sven Poullard 4-6 0-0 10, Josh Smith 1-1 1-2 3, Nilton Goodwin 0-1 0-0 0, Brandon Washington 0-1 0-0 0. **Totals** 29-62 7-15 69.
LEESVILLE (18-8, 5-0)
Eric Woods 8-16 0-0 18, Marcus Johnson 6-12 4-4 17, Chris Campbell 7-11 2-4 16, James Carter 1-1 1-2 3, Walter Mason 0-1 0-0 0, Johnnie Hearns 0-1 0-0 0, Jonathan Hopkins 5-12 2-2 12, Aaron Moore 3-6 1-2 7, Dennis Joiner 0-0 0-0 0, Onterrio Agnew 0-0 1-3 1, Sam Burley 0-0 0-0 0, Chris Elkins 0-0 1-2 1, Gabe Wilson 0-0 0-0 0. **Totals** 30-60 12-19 75.
Crowley .... 15 11 14 29—69
Leesville .... 21 14 28 12—75
Three-point goals—Crowley 4-10 (Allen 1-2, Morgan 0-1, Moore 1-2, Poullard 2-3, Goodwin 0-1, Washington 0-1) Leesville 3-15 (Woods 2-6, Johnson 1-2, Campbell 0-1, Hearns 0-1, Hopkins 0-5). **Rebounds**—Crowley 34 (Perkins 13) Leesville 29 (Campbell 7) **Assists**—Crowley 16 (Allen 5) Leesville 14 (Campbell 4). **Steals**—Crowley 11 (Allen 3) Leesville 22 (Woods 6).

Leesville 77, DeRidder 58
DERIDDER (18-5, 1-1)
D.J. Snow 0-8 0-0 0, Andre Herron 4-9 2-4 11, Ramel Handy 3-7 1-4 10, Jeff Jones 3-7 5-10 11, Julian Young 3-5 2-3 8, Tom Coody 1-3 0-2 2, Mark Simmons 3-9 3-4 10, Marques Manuel 0-1 2-2 2, Jamaal Jackson 0-1 4-4 4, Jason Kwok 0-0 0-0 0, Chris Brown 0-0 0-0 0, Travis Eaglin 0-0 0-0 0. **Totals** 17-50 19-33 58.
LEESVILLE (15-8, 2-0)
Chris Campbell 7-17 7-12 23, Eric Woods 11-17 5-9 29, James Carter 0-0 1-3 1, Walter Mason 1-5 0-0 2, Marcus Johnson 4-9 6-6 14, Aaron Moore 1-2 0-0 2, Johnnie Hearns 0-4 0-0 0, Jonathan Hopkins 3-6 0-0 6, Dennis Joiner 0-1 0-0 0. **Totals** 27-61 19-30 77.
DeRidder .... 10 9 26 13—58
Leesville .... 19 21 21 16—77
Three-point goals—DeRidder 5-19 (Snow 0-4, Herron 1-1, Handy 3-7, Coody 0-2, Simmons 1-5) Leesville 4-15 (Campbell 2-2, Woods 2-5, Mason 0-3, Johnson 0-2, Hearns 0-1, Joiner 0-1, Hopkins 0-1). **Rebounds**—DeRidder 31 (Jones 11) Leesville 41 (Woods 16). **Assists**—DeRidder 9 (Snow, Handy 3) Leesville 10 (Woods, Mason 3) **Steals**—DeRidder 4 (Snow 2) Leesville 9 (Campbell 4).

Bobcats .... 6 17 12 14 -49
Leesville ...... 13 12 19 20 -64

CATS (49)
Josh Thibodeaux 5 (4), 4-7 26, Tommy Viges 3, 1-1, 7, John Guillory 1(2), 2-2, 10, Titus Thomas 0, 2-2, 2, Josh Neville 1, 0-0, 2, Corey Woods 1, 0-2, 2, Kyle Savant 1, 0-2, 2. Totals 11 (6), 9-16 49.

WAMPUS CATS (64)
Chris Campbell 5, 8-13, 18, Eric Woods 6 (2), 6-7, 24, Johnnie Hearns 1, 0-0, 2, Walter Mason 0, 0-2, 0, Marcus Johnson 7 (1), 3-3, 20. Totals 19 (3), 17-25, 64.

Total Fouls Bobcats 18, Wampus Cats 14
Technicals Viges Eunice
Fouled out - Savant - Eunice
Records Cats (10-13, 3-3) Wampus Cats (NA, 6-0)

Leesville players celebrate

Leesville's James Carter raises Jonathan Hopkins onto his shoulders after the Leesville Wampus Cats beat the Woodlawn Panthers, 74-65, Saturday night to claim the Class 4A state title in the LHSAA Top 28 at the Cajundome in Lafayette. It was the first state title for Leesville. Please see stories, more photos, B-1, B-6.

Douglas Collier
— Staff photographer

Wampus Cats down Salmen; to meet STM

By Daniel Green
Sports Editor

For most of the year, Eric Woods and Chris Campbell have carried the offensive load for the Leesville Wampus Cats.

But Friday night against Salmen, they got a little help.

"Our teammates rallied around Eric and me," Campbell said following Leesville's 58-51 Class 4A regional victory over the Salmen Spartans Friday night.

"When Eric and I stepped up and took over the game, our teammates were right there along with us."

Down 38-30 with 1:25 remaining in the third quarter, Aaron Moore connected on a putback to spark a 9-0 run over the next 1:45 to give Leesville a 39-38 advantage early on in the fourth quarter.

A three-pointer by Jesse Carlin put Salmen back on top at 41-38 only to see Leesville score five straight points to regain the edge.

Garry Polk scored on a layup for Salmen to tie the game at 43-43, but the Wampus Cats (25-8) used a 10-2 surge, getting points from Marcus Johnson, Moore and Jonathan Hopkins to put the Cats up by eight points at 53-45 with 2:10 to go.

But Salmen wasn't done as Jesse Martin hit a three-pointer 20 seconds later to bring the Spartans to within five with 1:39 remaining in the contest.

However, Leesville scored five straight points on a layup by Woods, a free throw from Campbell and a pair from the charity stripe by Johnnie Hearns late in the game to put the Cats in control at 58-48.

Carlin hit a late three, but it wasn't enough as Leesville got the win.

"As a senior, I felt I had to step it up a level, especially since it is the playoffs," Campbell said. "It is my job to be a leader on the team and I just did what I am supposed to do."

Early on the Cats fell behind 7-3, but Hopkins and Campbell lifted Leesville to a 12-11 lead before a Josh Surette bucket late in the first put Salmen up by one at 13-12 going into the second quarter.

The Spartans (22-10) were able to build a four-point advantage during the second on a number of occasions, only to see Leesville rally to take a 26-24 lead with 1:11 to go on two free throws by Woods.

But Michael Timmons, who dominated the inside for Salmen in the first half, scored two buckets late in the first half to put the Spartans up 28-26 at the halftime intermission.

Leesville tied up the game to open the second half as Hopkins made a layup following a steal. But Salmen responded with a 10-2 run to take a 38-30 advantage late in the third period.

That is when the Wampus Cats took control and never looked back, using their pressure defense to seal the victory.

Woods led the Cats with 17 points and nine rebounds while Campbell finished with 13 points, eight boards, four assists and three steals.

Hopkins chipped in with eight points while Johnson and Moore came in with seven and six, respectively.

Carlin paced the Spartans with 18 points while Martin and Timmons finished with 11 and 10 points, respectively.

The Wampus Cats will take on the St. Thomas More Cougars this week in the Class 4A quarterfinals in Lafayette, most likely Friday night.

The Cougars defeated Bossier 59-47 Friday night in a regional contest.

However, Campbell believes that he and his teammates can beat anyone they play if they play Wampus Cat basketball.

"If we play our game, then I think we can win, regardless of who we play," he said. "We'll just have to handle the ball well and make our free throws and we will be alright."

If Leesville knocks off St. Thomas More next week, then it will be on to the Cajun-Dome for the Top 28 the following week, also in Lafayette.

Leesville tops St. Thomas More, 67-63
Cats to face Carver Monday at 8:30 p.m. in CajunDome

By Daniel Green
Sports Editor

LAFAYETTE — It's a shot where no one is guarding you or even allowed to get near you.

So why is a free throw so hard to make?

The St. Thomas More Cougars may be asking that question right now as they connected on just five of 15 free throw attempts while Leesville made 23 of 33 for the game as the Wampus Cats came away with a 67-63 victory Friday night in a Class 4A quarterfinal contest.

Leesville (26-8) returns to the Top 28 for the second straight year and will play against the Carver Rams out of New Orleans at 8:30 p.m. Monday night in the Cajun-Dome on the campus of the University of Louisiana-Lafayette. No tickets will be available at the LHS office, but they will be on sale at the event for $7 per person.

Leading by no more than six at any time in the game, Leesville managed to maintain the lead throughout the game despite some timely three-point shooting by the Cougars, who finished the season at 26-8.

The Wampus Cat owned a 32-27 advantage at the halftime break thanks to a pair of free throws by Marcus Johnson, but Seth Hayes hit a pair of three-pointers while teammates Sims Bruns added one of his own during an 11-2 St. Thomas More run to open the second half, pushing the Cougars out to a 38-34 lead about midway through the third quarter.

Chris Campbell nailed a pair of free throws to stop the Cougar surge momentarily, only to see 6-9 Abray Milson bring down the house with an emphatic slam dunk just a few seconds later to put St. Thomas More ahead by four at 40-36.

But the enthusiasm of the crowd was short-lived as Johnson buried a three-pointer and Eric Woods sank a short jumper, sparking a quarter-ending 10-3 run by the Wampus Cats, giving Leesville a 46-43 lead heading into the final period of regulation.

Hayes knocked home a three to tie the score to open the fourth, but Leesville used a quick 6-3 spurt to go back up by three points at 52-49 on a layup by Woods.

The Cats maintained their three-point edge until Chris Cortese bombed in a three-pointer with two minutes to go, tying the game at 56-56.

But Leesville's Aaron Moore would score following a missed free throw while Johnnie Hearns and Johnson each hit a pair of free throws during a 6-1 push, giving the Cats a 62-57 lead with 54 seconds left in the game.

Cortese pulled STM to within two at 62-60 with his second three-pointer of the quarter but three of four free throws by Leesville upped the lead back to five points with just 15 seconds to go.

Hayes would hit an acrobatic three-pointer with six seconds to go in the game to cut the deficit to two points, but Campbell sealed the deal for the Cats with a pair of free throws with 4.8 seconds left to secure the victory for Leesville.

"We made our free throws down the stretch and they didn't," said Campbell following the game. "That's all you can really say. We played big on defense in the second half and we finished it off with our free throws."

The Cats made 11 of 13 free throws during the final eight minutes of the contest while St. Thomas More ended up two for six in the fourth period.

"We had confidence that we could make the shots late and we believed in ourselves," Woods said. "It feels really good to win and I am glad that we have the opportunity to go back to the Top 28."

But for every second of the 32-minute game, it wasn't certain who would win the game, only that it would most likely go down to the wire.

The two teams exchanged the lead five times in the first quarter and it appeared as if Leesville had opened up a 12-9 lead with just under to minutes to go when Campbell hit a driving shot in the lane.

See CATS, P. 3B

Set for the Cougars

The Leesville Wampus Cat basketball team is one win away from making a second consecutive trip to the Top 28. Leesville will travel to meet St. Thomas More today at 7 p.m. in Lafayette in a Class 4A quarterfinal game. Among the players who see action for the Cats are Aaron Moore (photo at left) and Marcus Johnson (photo at right). Advance tickets for the contest are on sale at the Leesville High School office. Tickets for the game cost $5 per person.

Leader photos/Curtis Knight

Class 4A semifinals
Leesville 61, Carver 54

CARVER (29-9)
Bruce Edwards 1-5 1-3 3, Terry Simon 6-10 0-0 14, Dwon Robinson 1-1 1-2 3, Damien Sawyer 3-4 0-0 6, Johnny Anderson 0-3 0-1 0, Jemart Miller 3-9 3-4 10, Billy Espedron 0-0 0-0 0, Jason ALexander 0-0 0-0 0, Howard Mullen 0-0 0-0 0, Micheal Jackson 0-0 0-0 0, Lionel Green 0-2 2-2 2, D'Sean Young 0-1 0-0 0, Rickey Woods 6-8 4-6 16. Totals 20-43 11-20 54.

LEESVILLE (27-8)
Eric Woods 5-15 7-8 18, Chris Campbell 8-16 5-6 21, Jonathan Hopkins 0-2 0-0 0, Marcus Johnson 3-7 4-5 10, James Carter 0-0 1-2 1, Johnnie Hearns 1-3 4-4 7, Chris Elkins 0-0 0-0 0, Gabe Wilson 0-0 0-0 0, Walter Mason 0-0 0-0 0, Dennis Joiner 0-0 0-0 0, Onterrio Agnew 0-0 0-0 0, Aaron Moore 1-1 2-2 4, Sam Burley 0-0 0-0 0. Totals 18-44 23-27 61.

CARVER	19	17	8	10	— 54
LEESVILLE	10	21	12	18	— 61

Three-point goals—Carver 3-11 (Simon 2-5, Miller 1-4, Edwards 0-2), Leesville 2-12 (Hearns 1-2, Woods 1-5, Hopkins 0-1, Campbell 0-2, Johnson 0-2). Fouled out—Edwards, R.Woods. Rebounds—Carver 30 (Simon, Woods 7), Leesville 27 (Woods, Campbell 6). Assists—Carver 8 (Simon 3), Leesville 8 (Campbell 3). Total fouls—Carver 26, Leesville 18. A—4,915.

Leesville players celebrate

Leesville's James Carter raises Jonathan Hopkins onto his shoulders after the Leesville Wampus Cats beat the Woodlawn Panthers, 74-65, Saturday night to claim the Class 4A state title in the LHSAA Top 28 at the Cajundome in Lafayette. It was the first state title for Leesville. Please see stories, more photos, B-1, B-6.

Douglas Collier — Staff photographer

FINALS

Short turnaround leaves coaches short of information

By Dan McDonald
Gannett News Service

LAFAYETTE — The hazards of playing on the opening night of the Top 28 state prep basketball tournament were brought into focus by two of the Class 3A coaches Monday night.

Rayville beat Landry in a 55-53 nail-biter in Monday's second game, and both coaches talked after the game about how difficult it was to prepare for an unfamiliar opponent so quickly after Friday's quarterfinals.

"We didn't know who their shooters were," said Landry coach Curtis Moore. "It took us the first quarter to find out."

"Both of us played on Friday night, and there was no school on Saturday or Sunday," said Rayville coach Larry Wilson. "All we had was school phone numbers and not home numbers. Both of us pretty much went into it blind ... we know very little about each other."

With the quick turnaround between games, there was little opportunity for any of the opening-night coaches to view videotapes of Monday semifinal opponents.

"We knew a little about their personnel," said Moore, "but we didn't know any of their schemes."

ALMOST SWEET REVENGE

One year ago, it was Minden that held a big lead in its Class 3A semifinal against St. James, only to have the Wildcats rally in the final minute in taking a 63-60 victory.

On Monday night, St. James held a double-digit lead against the Crimson Tide with just over two minutes left.

"I thought it maybe was our turn," said Minden head coach Alan Shaw.

Minden rallied in those final two minutes and got within three points with 39 seconds left, and then missed a 3-pointer that could have tied the game with just over 15 seconds left. The Tide got a rebound and a dunk to cut it to one, but did not have time to get off a game-winner after St. James missed a pair of free throws with 3.8 seconds left.

"We knew there was a revenge factor," said St. James head coach Lionel Enidore. "We knew it wouldn't be easy."

WESTERCHIL STYLIN'

The opening night fashion award went to Leesville head coach Grant Westerchil, who wore a multi-color patchwork vest during the Wampus Cats' Class 4A semifinal battle with Carver.

Maybe his players were distracted, since Carver jumped in front 8-0 and led by as many as 13 points early in the second quarter before Leesville rallied to make it much closer at halftime.

Westerchil tired of runner-up role

Bruce M. Vierguiz
Louisiana Gannett News

LAFAYETTE — Leesville coach Grant Westerchil has experienced joy and sorrow in his three appearances at the boys Top 28 state basketball tournament.

In 1996, Westerchil's first trip to the Top 28, the 6-foot-6 coach took a knee before the Wampus Cats' Class 4A semifinal game with St. Thomas More and proposed to his then-fiancée Beth.

Beth accepted the proposal, and Leesville went on to win 76-74 in overtime.

Westerchil's team still finished as the bridesmaid, losing to Cohen 77-63 in the title game.

"Every time I see a picture of the place I think about my proposal," mused Westerchil. "I should hang a picture of the Assembly Center on my wall, but people would probably say, 'What's that up there for?'"

But the '96 team, according to Westerchil, was the most talented team he has taken to the Top 28.

That team included McNeese State's Demond Mallet, plus UL-Lafayette's Reggie DeGray and Lonnie Thomas.

"I thought we were going to win it that year," said Westerchil. "We just didn't handle the ball well."

Westerchil vowed that the Wampus Cats would be back, and they made it last year, taking on a Chris Duhon led Salmen team in the semifinals.

Once again, the Wampus Cats prevailed, downing Salmen 78-75 to set up a meeting with top-ranked Peabody.

Once again, Leesville came up short, dropping a 79-60 decision to the Warhorses.

"I thought maybe we'd play them closer because we only lost to them by three points early in the season," said Westerchil, "but Peabody had the better team."

But resiliency is still paying dividends for the Wampus Cats.

Although most doubted they would get back to the Top 28 after losing three starters, including first-team all-stater Darnell Bradley, the Wampus Cats (27-6) are back once more.

Leesville can win that elusive first state boys basketball championship by beating second-ranked Woodlawn of Baton Rouge (34-3) in the 4A title game starting at 7 tonight at the Cajundome.

"I'd say this group has a special quality to it," said Westerchil. "We just started out trying to make some noise in the playoffs. But we've had some luck, and the kids have found a way to win in every playoff game we've had."

The Wampus Cats know they will have to do the same against favored Woodlawn.

STATE CHAMPIONS

Leesville wins 4A title, loses coach

By Bruce M. Viergutz
Staff reporter

LAFAYETTE — Its coach will be gone after this season, but the thrill of winning the school's first boys' state basketball championship may never leave for Leesville.

Fueled by Chris Campbell's 28 points and 22 by Eric Woods, the seventh-ranked Wampus Cats made history by downing second-ranked Woodlawn of Baton Rouge, 74-65, to win the Class 4A state championship Saturday night at the Top 28 at the Cajundome. Leesville finished second last season and in 1995.

"This has been a dream come true for me," said Woods, who was named the 4A Most Valuable Player by the working media. "There is nothing else like it."

The victory was somewhat bittersweet for the Wampus Cats, who learned that their head coach Grant Westerchil is resigning. Westerchil has been at Leesville for seven years.

"Leesville basketball isn't about me," said Westerchil, who broke down in the locker room when he told the players of his decision. "Leesville basketball is about the kids."

Westerchil then joked: "I didn't tell them before the game, but I was saving it in case we were behind at halftime and I needed a Knute Rockne speech."

No such dialogue was needed.

Leesville (28-8), which led 32-27 at intermission, got seven points from Campbell and three from Woods to spark a 10-5 run to begin the third quarter. Campbell, who finished as the third leading scorer in the tournament with 49 points, put the Wampus Cats on top, 42-32, after a free throw with 5:17 left in the third.

Woodlawn (34-4) cut the deficit to four points twice in the second half, the last coming when Darnell Lazare hit a turnaround jumper to pull the Panthers within 58-54 with 3:04 remaining in the game.

But Campbell scored five straight points to put Leesville up 63-54 and the Wampus Cats hit 9 of 14 free throws in the final 2:17.

Leesville connected on 20 of 26 free throws for the game.

"My kids finally learned that you can put a team away by hitting your free throws," said Westerchil, who earlier this year compared the Wampus Cats' free throw shooting to a Little Dribblers' team. "But not any more. I just stopped getting on them about it and they started to hit them with some consistency."

Woodlawn, which as finished state runners-up in 1968 before winning the 4A title the following year, was led by James Collins and Jerimie Collier with 17 points each. Kendrick Barber added 13.

"Congratulations to Leesville, they played a great game," said Woodlawn coach Kenny Almond. "That's especially true for (Woods). He showed the kind of player he is. He's hard to guard and he had one heck of a night for them.

"I was talking to the Salmen coach and he told me he plays like Magic Johnson. He's obviously not as good, but like Magic, he does everything. He can shoot, penetrate, dribble and handle the ball."

Almond felt his Panthers gave a great effort despite the loss.

"We just had some things go wrong that hadn't gone wrong all year," said Almond. "It's like I said Tuesday; we were playing a team determined to win. They had a purpose to everything they did tonight."

The only other state title won by Leesville came in 1976 when the boys claimed a state track championship. The Wampus Cats ended the season with a 16-game winning streak.

"I've had teams with more talent," said Westerchil, "but I've never had one this special. I love them and I will miss them."

Bruce M. Viergutz 487-6367; bviergutz@thetowntalk.com

> "I've had teams with more talent, but I've never had one this special. I love them and I will miss them."
> — Grant Westerchil, Leesville coach

Douglas Collier — Staff photographer

Leesville's Chris Campbell puts an exclamation mark on the Wampus Cats' 74-65 victory Saturday night over Woodlawn to win the Class 4A state championship. Campbell finished with 28 points.

Leesville defeats Woodlawn for Class 4A title

Westerchil calls it quits after getting win

BY ADAM BURNS
AMERICAN PRESS

LAFAYETTE — Eric Woods knew how to jump start the Leesville Wampus Cats Saturday night. Senior guard Chris Campbell and coach Grant Westerchil knew how to finish their respective high school careers in style.

Woods scored 12 of his 22 points in the first quarter and Campbell helped stave off several Woodlawn Baton Rouge runs in the second half as Leesville won its first boys basketball state championship, beating the Panthers for the Class 4A crown 74-65 here at the Cajundome.

It was the first state title for Leesville in any sport not involving hurdles or shot puts. The only other title in school history was the boys track and field crown in 1978.

Westerchil, who has been runner-up twice, confirmed he was leaving coaching after winning a title in his third try.

"If being runner up is like kissing your sister, this is like kissing my wife," said Westerchil, who is leaving coaching to enter the insurance business. "If you had asked me in December who was going to win it all I would have said not us. The only problem now is I promised to shave my head if we won it this year."

"Eric Woods showed the kind of player he was and I thought Leesville showed the kind of determination we showed when we won it in 1999 after losing the last time," Woodlawn coach Kenny Almond said. "Leesville is a very good team, they wouldn't have been here if they weren't, but we were not only playing against their talent but their persistence. They were playing with a purpose about them in everything they did."

In addition to Woods' 22, Campbell finished with a game-high 28 and Marcus Johnsen added 11. Woods also pulled down 10 rebounds and was named the games' MVP. Campbell hit 8 of 11 shots and was 11-for-11 from the free throw line.

"Those three have done it all year long," Westerchil said. "We have great

McNeil tops Minden in 2A championship PAGE D7

See LEESVILLE, Page D3

LEESVILLE: Defeats Woodlawn-BR for Class 4A title

from PAGE D1

role players, but I want these three to shoot it; the other guys I'm like, 'shoot it if you can't get it to these three.'"

After spending most of the first half in foul trouble, Campbell scored 18 of his 28 points in the second half, including a pair of key buckets late in the fourth quarter. Trailing the entire game, Woodlawn cut the deficit to 58-54 on a post up move by Darnell Lazarre.

But Campbell was fouled making a layup on the ensuing play, made the free throw, and then threw down a two-fisted slam dunk keyed by a Marcus Johnson steal to give the Wampus Cats a comfortable margin with 2:40 remaining.

"I was kind of surprised they put their 6-6 guys on me when all I do is penetrate," Campbell said. "But in the second half I just kept trying to be aggressive. I knew we couldn't just sit on a lead and hope they wouldn't come back."

Leesville scored on eight of its first nine possessions, but Woodlawn's 3-point shooting and four blocks by Karandick Ogunride kept the Panthers in striking distance. A 3-pointer by Kendrick Barber with less than a minute remaining in the second quarter sent Leesville to the locker room leading 32-27.

Except for a spurt in the third quarter where Woodlawn forward Jerarrie Collier scored nearly every time he touched the ball, none of the Panthers could get going offensively.

Woodlawn shot 4-of-7 from the three-point line in the first half, but made only 2-of-15 in the second.

"It was kind of frustrating," Almond said. "We had some things go wrong that hadn't really gone wrong for us all year, at least not at the same time. And those Leesville guys are really hard to defend."

Collier scored 15 of his 17 points in the third. The Panthers leading scorer James Collins scored 17 points, but was only 3-for-11 from the field.

"The shots I took felt good they just went in and out," Collier said. "We worked so hard to get here, I didn't expect this to happen."

Woods, Davis make Top 28 All-Tourney team

LAFAYETTE (AP) — Marcus Spears of Southern Lab, who led the Kittens to their 12th state championship, was selected as the Most Valuable Player of the Top 28 Tournament which concluded Saturday at the Cajundome.

Spears was joined on the team by Kyle Jones of Family Christian, Byron Williams of McCall, Eric Woods of Leesville, Joey Armstrong of Dubach, Tim Bush of Shaw, Tyrone Johnson of Rayville, Cedric Davis of Many, Donald Perry of McCall, Kaye Gonzales of Family Christian, Ryan Martin of Jesuit, Chad Barnes of Jesuit and Chris Campbell of Leesville.

The tournament finished its final day with a total attendance of 40,974, the seventh straight year that the tournament topped 40,000 in attendance and the 10th highest total in the 41-year history of the event.

Teams in Pictures

This section of the book is meant to provide as much documentation of LHS basketball teams as possible. While the narrtive portion of the history provides quick reviews and highlights key moments and key players and coaches, this section is here simply to chronicle what could be found in terms of the teams who suited up to play bsketball in the black and gold.

No excuses or caveats are offered up, but an explanaiton is in order. As has been stated in other parts of the book, there is no consistent standard in terms of documenting what happened in this, or any other sport at LHS or at any other sport. Principals change, Yearbook Sponsors change, certainly the students who create and edit the yearbooks change. By and large, things are consistent within 2 -3 years in any direction of any year, but when you move from decade to decade, there are signfiicant changes in what was documented, and thus recorded.

The pictures you see in this section come primarily from LHS yearbooks. In the 50s, 60s, and 70s, team pictures were key components of yearbooks. Things changed in the 80s to a degree. Also, FINDING a yearbook is not always easy. We did the best we could. If you see a year where no team picture is presented, some picture or groups of pictures were crafted together. Sometimes, we couldn't find ANY pictures, so we used newspaper stories or All-District results to document the teams. No one, no team, no players and no event was intentionally left out of this effort. If we could find it, we put in these pages. We did our best and our goal was to document LHS basketball, for boys and for girls.

Whe we could find documentation of who was IN the picture, we provided it. Nothing was intentionally ommitted.

1950

BOY'S BASKETBALL TEAM

First row: Charles Roebuck, Hubert Williams—Co-Captain, Bobby Mooney, Hank Berwick, Roy Pelt, Truman Ellis. Second row: Emerson Singletary, Lynn Lee, Delmon Craft, Jim Beltz, Marion Patterson. Third row: Sonny Nessmith, Bill Beavers, J. L. Smith, Edward Williams—Captain, James Bolgiano, Mr. Z. Stiles—Coach. (Missing when picture was made: B. A. Gill and Max Hill.)

Boys' Record: 18-5

GIRL'S BASKETBALL TEAM

First row: Jane Carey, Virginia Self, Audrey Chamberlain, Louise Harvey, L. D. Bynog, Janice Ellis, Gladys Helen Lewis, Joy Ann Scogin, Faye Jeane. Second row: Jean Hickman, Gwendolyn Whittaker, Georgia Fay Haymon, Betty Paddy, Ellen Cooley, Norma Chance, Helen Cooley—Captain, Annette Norris—Co-Captain, Mr. A. L. Temple—Coach.

Girls' Record: 21-7

1951

Boys' Record: Unknown

THURSDAY, MARCH 15, 1951

Leesville Girls State Class "A" Runner-up

The Leesville High School Wampuscats girls basketball team advanced to the finals of the Louisiana High School Basketball Tournament held in Hammond, La this past weekend.

The Leesville girls have amassed a spectacular sum of 2,249 points in forty-nine games while allowing their opponents to only 1,524.

The Kittenettes have compiled an amazing record of some forty two wins in their forty-nine contests which includes the state and district tournament. Only two losses this year were handed the Cats in scheduled contests while five were lost in tournaments.

The Leesville Kittenettes have taken six tournaments while placing second in four, plus the state and district tournaments.

The Cats were led by forward Audrey Chamberlain who has flipped in 1281 points, Betty Paddy another scoring ace was second in the point column but was closely followed by Marie Arnold. Other forwards who saw much action this year are Norma Chance and L. D. Bynog who played as guard. On the opposite side of the court are tall Jane Carey, Reliable Joy Ann Scogin and fast Faye Jeane.

Only two Wampus Cats will not return next year; they are, Captain Joy Ann Scogin, Co-captain Norma Chance.

At the District tournament held at McNeese State College in Lake Charles the Cats downed a hapless St. Charles sextet of Lake Charles 61-16 to annex the district crown.

The Cats came through brilliantly at the State Tournament held at Southwestern Louisiana College at Hammond, by opening things up with a 2-0 forfeit victory over Farmerville and then going on to defeat Many 49-38, and Scott 58-49.

The Leesville Girls put up a good fight the first half in the (Continued on Back Page)

Leesville Girls
(Continued From Page One)

finals but were soon overcome by the much taller lassies from Oak Grove who showed their experience and wound things up with a decisive 37-19 victory over the Cats.

The Girls under the able mentorship of A. L. Temple, gathered some consolation by placing two on the All-Star squad. The Girls who reached the dream team were forward Betty Paddy and Jane Carey.

Much praise goes to Mr Temple for his fine job of coaching these girls to one of the most coveted positions in Louisiana Basketball.

Girls' Record 42-7; State Runner-Up

1952

Back Row: Jim Beltz, Guard; Haddox Bolgiano, Forward; Robert Freeman, Forward; Kenneth Smith, Center; Earl Holt, Center; Coach Zolon Stiles.

Middle Row: Mike Moss, Guard; Jerry Craft, Forward; Eugene Ammons, Guard; Alton Herring, Guard; Marvin Parker, Guard; Ted Paris, Guard; Doy Dunham, Guard.

Front Row: Jack Ward, Forward; George Stanly, Forward; Ed Parker, Forward; Robert Moss, Guard; Larry Goins, Guard; Joe Howard, Forward; James Cloessner, Forward.

Boys' Record: 2-10

Back Row: Peggy Montgomery, Guard; Gwendolyn Whittaker, Guard; Marie Arnold, Forward; Shirley Cavanaugh, Forward; Doris Paddy, Forward; Guinell Smart, Coach; Bettye Cryer, Mgr.

Middle Row: Audrey Chamberlain, Forward; Betty Paddy, Forward; Jane Carey, Guard; June Williams, Guard; Louise Harvey, Guard; Annette Norris, Forward.

First Row: Gelena Scoggins, Guard; Gladys Helen Lewis, Guard; Jean Jones, Guard; Sherry Hardwick, Guard; Faye Jeane, Guard; Joy Beth Bolgiano, Guard.

Girls' Record: 16-2

_1953_

EBER SANDELL Guard	LARRY GOINS Guard	BILLY BENNETT Coach

Wins - 27
Losses - 15
Total Points Scored:
  Leesville - 1,743
  Opponents - 1,513
Average Points per game:
  Leesville - 42.0
  Opponents - 36.1

*District Tourney
**State Tourney
TOURNAMENT RESULTS
First Place - Simpson
Second Place - Hornbeck
Second Place - Leesville
Third Place - District
Champions of District - 1-A

Class A' All-State Selections

Boys
Travis Ford, Jonesboro, forward.
Harmon Ayres, Jonesboro, forward.
Star Stumpf, Newman, center.
Leon Greenblatt, Newman, guard.
Ralph Richardson, Springhill, guard.
Eber Sandlin, Leesville, center.
John Crowe, Springhill, center.
Earl McClain, Covington, guard.
Phinn Kennon, Jena, center.
Bobby Booth, Hammond, center.

Girls
..First team.
Forwards — Glenda Bennett, Winnsboro, Ann Crawford, Winnsboro, Gretchan Kovac, Oak Grove.
Guards—Gwendolyn Whittaker, Leesville; Mitzie Roberts, Winnfield; Yvonne Cromwell, LaSalle.
Second team:
Forwards — Mary Trahant, Amite; Shirley Hayers, Many; Audrey Chamberlain, Leesville.
Guards — Beth Landry, Mt. Carmel of Lafayette; Dorothy Williams, Winnsboro; Faye Jeane, Leesville.

BASKETBALL

Mrs. Susan
Coach

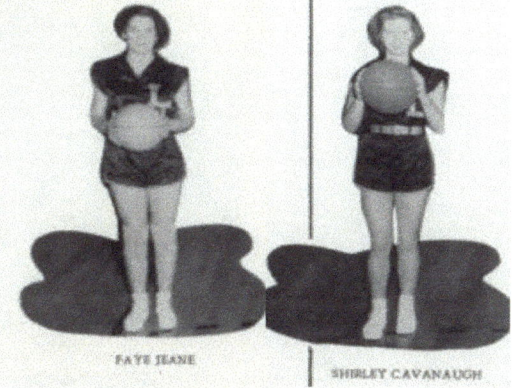

FAYE JEANE   SHIRLEY CAVANAUGH

RECORD FOR SEASON:
Games Won - 36
Games Lost - 1
Total points scored:
  Leesville 1,530
  Opponents   726

TOURNAMENT RESULTS:
First Place - Anacoco
First Place - Simpson
First Place - Leesville
First Place - District-Class A
First Place - District Conference
Third Place - State-Class A
District Grand Champions

_1954_

Boys' Record 28-14; District Champions

1954 Lady Wampus Cats, State Runner-Up, 29-1

RECORD FOR SEASON	TOURNAMENT RESULTS
Games won - 29	First Place - Hornbeck
Games lost - 1	First Place - Rosepine
Total points scored:	First Place - Leesville
Leesville - 1468	First Place - District 6-A
Opponents - 711	Second Place - State Tourney
	Grand Champions - Central La.
	Central La. Champions

ALL STATE PLAYERS

FORWARDS	GUARDS
Audrey Truax	Faye Jeane
Shirley Cavanaugh	Gwen Whittaker

1955

RECORD FOR SEASON

Games won - 28
Games lost - 11
          39

TOTAL POINTS SCORED

Leesville - 1980
Opponents - 1575

TOURNAMENT RESULTS

LEESVILLE TOURNEY - First Place
PITKIN TOURNEY - Second Place

Co-Captains
DON GOINS - JIMMY EDWARDS

JIMMY EDWARDS - Forward and Center   DON GOINS - Guard

Boys' Record: 28-13

Girls' Basketball

Girls' Record: 9-16

1956

Boys Record: 20-13

Girls' Record: 13-6

1957

Boys Record: 10-10

State Quarter-Finalist

Girls' Record: 15-6

1958

Boys' Record: 24-10

1957-58 WAMPUS CAT TEAM

Girls' Record: Unknown

1959

Boys' Record: 20-14

L-R Front Row: Jody Westmoreland, Kay Vandergriff, Judy Cavanaugh (Captain), Linda Deon, Kathleen Moore, Kay Kitchen
Middle Row: Cheryl Kile, Margaret Williams, Janice St. John, Carolyn Gormley, Karolyn Holifield (Captain), Mary Nell Hall, Carol Adamson.
Back Row: Betty Cavanaugh, Mary Gray (Manager), Sharon Moore, Mrs. Agatha Rhodes (coach) Coleen Young, Janie Jones (Manager), Dorothy Davis.

Girls' Record: Unknown

1960

VARSITY TEAM and MANAGER CHARLES CULOTTA

Boys' Record 19-16

Varsity Basketball Team and Managers

Girls' Record: 10-14

1961

A VALUABLE PLAYER

Richard Reese has made many accomplishments in basketball during his stay at Leesville High School. Among his achievements are his selection to the 3-AA All-District First team, AA All-Southwest Louisiana third team of 1960. During this time he set a new school record of the most points scored in a season, and finished among the top scorers in La. on average per game basis.

In the 1960-61 season, he again established himself as an outstanding player by breaking the school and conference record for the most points scored in a game, with 42 points against Jena. Richard finished the regular season with an average of 23.6 points per game in 35 games and an average of 27.6 points per game in conference competition.

Although honors have not been given out, it is felt that Richard is in line for consideration of many.

STATISTICS

Games played	35
Games won	28
Games lost	7
Total points scored	2339
Total points against	1814
Offensive average	66.8
Defensive average	54.6

Tournaments:
- First Place
  - Leesville
  - Anacoco
  - Evans
  - DeRidder
- Second Place
  - Tioga
  - Central La. Rally
- Third Place
  - District 3-AA

THE SQUAD

Boys' Record: 28-7

1961

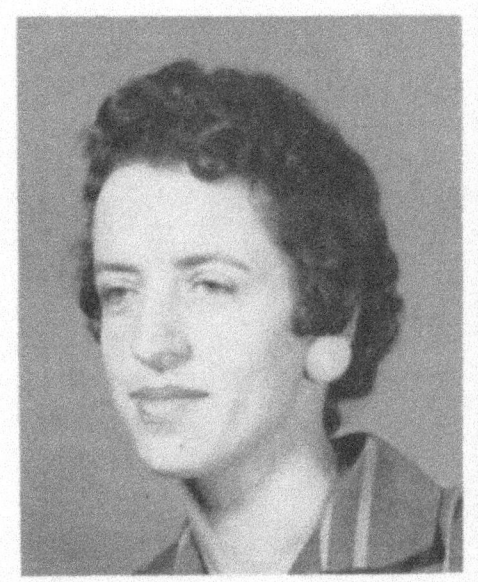

COACH

Miss Gotreaux

COLEEN YOUNG
Basketball

Season Record: Unknown

Last Year of Girls Basketball Until 1975

1962

Boys' Record 10-18

1963

Boys' Record: 2 – 24

1964

Boys' Record: 16-8

_1965_

THE VARSITY

Boys' Record 15-11

1966

Boys' Record: 8-10

1967

1966-67 "Wampus Cat" Basketball Team

Boys' Record: 17-17

1968

Boys' Record: 15-17

1969

Boys' Record: 22-10

1970

Boys' Record: 23-11, District Champions

1971

Boys' Record: 15-16

1972

Boys Record: 6-22

1973

FIRST ROW: Billy Counts, Floyd Tinsley, Dino Brown, Ricky Shaw, Ken Hughes, Leland Bennett, Darrell Bynog, Steve Coffman. SECOND ROW: Coach Keith Andrews, Coach Curtis Brazil, Tracy Tinsley, John Hardin, Robert Walker, John Joiner, Johnny Walters, John Smart; Managers Terry Farris, Jerry Lee, Peter Addison, Sam Fulton.

Boys' Record: 20-15

1974

Boys' Record 24-13

1975

VARSITY: (L-r, top row), Head Basketball Coach Keith Andrews, Milton Clayton (mgr.), Brian Frederick (mgr.), Lawrence Joiner, John Joiner, Russell Murphy, Dexter Upshaw, Dennis Joiner, Sammy Bursh, Mike Boozer (mgr.), Robert Noel (mgr.), Assistant Coach Curtis Brazil. (Bottom row) Randall Smith, Deno Brown, Tracy Tinsley, Dennis Van Dine, Dennis Mayeaux, Raymond Smith.

Boys' Record, 30-7, District Champions

1976

Boys' Record: 16-19

LEESVILLE HIGH LADY CATS--For the First time in many years the Leesville High school will field a girls' basketball team this season. The team, coached by Billy Crawford, will open the 1975-76 season in Hornbeck tonight at 6:30. The team will play a 21-game schedule plus participate in three tournaments. Thursday, Friday and Saturday the squad will participate in the DeRidder tournament. District play for the Lady Cats will not open until December 30 when they host Oakdale. Other district opponents include Washington, Rayne, Jennings, Eunice, and West Lake, all in District 4-AAA. Members of the team include, left to right, bottom row, Kathy Tinsley, Etta Gabor, Debbie Strait, Cindy Fulda, Dottie Lucius, Barbara Stewart, Penny Potter, Susie Woodroff, Brenda Lee, Carolyn Matthews, Donna Saunders, Jenny Covington and Teola Crosby. Second row, left to right, Coach Crawford, Cindy White, Debbie Durett, Gwen Worfel, Lindsey Simms, Vera DeLos Santos, Nita Paris, Valerie Peel, Carol Hopper, Kim Beavers, Helen Youngblood, Tammy Mitchell, Silvia DeLos Santos, Linda Youngblood, statistician; and Cathy Clary, manager. Absent from the photograph are Barbara Bureau and Denise Davis.

Girls' Record: 11-13

1977

Varsity: Standing - L to R: Coach Burgess, Anthony Pratt, Russel Murphy, Robert Freshley, Cedric Johnson, Jerry Lynch, James Williams, Richard Bastedo, and Coach Mike Mallet. Kneeling - L to R: Mike Burgess, Terry Holt, Cordell Upshaw, Larry Averhart, Dennis Joiner, William Gardiner, Gerald Kerry, Ronnie Bouya, and Carlton Wilson.

Boys' Record: 21-12

Standing - L to R: Coach Billy Crawford, Faye Windham, Debbie Crosby, Debbie Nix, Debra Cage, Valerie Peel, Kim Beavers, Carolyn Matthews, Linda Youngblood, Sandra Barnett, and Cindy Broyles. Kneeling - L to R: Angela Walker, Bonnie Hobbs, Barbara Moore, Karen Edwards, Kay Mayeaux, Penny Potter, Teola Crosby, Kathy Tinsley, Vicki West and Carolyn Moore.

Girls Record: 6-16

1978

We're #1 — Standing L. to R. Coach Mallet, Ron Bouya, Richard Bastedo, Vernon Travis, Zeno Bursh, Robert Gaines, Mike McShane, Jerry Lynch, Robert Freshly, Cedric Johnson, Harold Tomas. Kneeling Jasper Keys, Rodney Simons, Gerald Kerry, Van Upshaw, James Rock, Jim Coburn, Keith Joiner, Steve Payton, Coach Culbreath.

Boys' Record: 21-10

Girls' Record: 0-20

1979

VARSITY WAMPUS CATS BASKETBALL 78-79

Top Row — Vernon Travis, Jimmy Johnson, Percy Gammage, Russell Neely, Robert Gaines, Richard Turner. Bottom Row — Matt Oliver, Levon White, Gerald Kerry, Leon Jackson, Sam Cox.

Boys' Record: 9-17

Most Valuable Player — Susan Skidmore
Coaches' Award — Dorothy Lipton
Most Improved Player — Coach Janet Manuel

Sue Skidmore
Sabrina Bursh
Dorthy Lipton

Girls' Record: 3-17

1980

Standing: Leon Jackson, Vernon Travis, Percy Gammage, Al Hunter, Undrea Johnson, Robert Gaines, Eric Travis, Michael Butler, Calvin Smith. Kneeling: Danny Bess, Levon White, Keith Joine, Sam Cox, Shelton Heckerson, Lester Hohnson, Robert Kennedy, Matt Oliver.

Boys' Record: 11-15

Girls Record: Unknown

1981

The 1980-81 Wampus Cats basketball team

Opening the 1980-81 Wampus Cats basketball season here Tuesday night in a non-district game against Marion High School of Lake Charles will be, from left, front, Calvin Smith, Cedric Upshaw, Robert Kennedy, Dewayne Smith, Steve Kennedy, Mark Haltberry and Shelton Hickerson. From left, second, will be Grady Norton, Eric Martin, Mike Butler, Nikita Wilson, Mark Freshley, Steve Travis, Eric Travis, Leon Jackson (co-captain) and Levon White (co-captain) (Leader Staff Photo by Cheryl Walker-Dych)

Boys' Record: 16-11

Ready for opener here Tuesday

Members of the 1980-81 Leesville High School girls basketball squad, who will open their season here Tuesday at five p.m. against Marion of Lake Charles, are, kneeling, from left, Regina Dixon and Monica Boerner (co-captains), and back row, from left, Shannon Conners, Jill Dowden, Cathy Ellis, Susan Scoggins, Barbara Johnson, Julie Taylor, Suzanne Kirk, Michelle Bowman, Regina Ragland, Fransie Sparks and Mary Lipton. (Leader Staff photo by Cheryl Walker-Dych)

Girls' Record: 8-12

1982

Boys' Record: 25-1, District Champions

The 1981-82 Lady Cats

Girls' Record: 16-7

1983

First Row: Meshelle Bowman, Connie Boerner (statisticians). Second Row, Kneeling: Garland Thomas, Matthew Woods, Doryl Jones, Ronald Seastrunk, Mark Holtsberry, Steve Kennedy, manager Donny Rowzee. Third Row: Coach Donny Smith, Head Coach Mike Mollet, Richard Smoor, Fitzgerald Crittle, James Jackson, Steve Travis, Nikito Wilson, Grant Westerchil, Grady Norton, Eric Martin, Matthew Miller, Coach Kay Taylor.

Boys' Record: 30-4, District Champions

Back Row, L to R: Faye Shaw, Dina Johnson, Connie Howard, Holly Wentz, Cynthia Faye Howard, Sheila Ford, Lowlette Powe, Coach Jordan. Front Row, L to R: Regina Dean, Michelle Hall, Lorenda Smartt, Vanessa Gordon, Tina Miller.

Girls Record: 3-18

1984

Row 1: Daniel Rowzee, Matthew Wood, Arnold McPhearson, Thomas Garland, Ronald Seastrunk, Wayne Palmer, Keith Hollands, Recoe Ragland, Jerry Howard, Michael Joiner. Row nedy, Tony Marshle, Fitz Crittle, Grant Westerchil, Marro Hawkens, Terry Cooper, Derrik Edwards, Darel Sparks, Danny Smith.

Boy's Record: 17-12

Row 1: Regina Deans, Carla Smith, Vanessa Gordon, Lorenda Smart, Michell Hall, Coach Patsy Raiford, Miller, Faye Shaw, Ginnie Freshley, Connie Howard, Kim Dowden, Dina Johnson, Shelia Ford.

Girls' Record: 12-10

1985

Boys' Record: 29-6, State Semi-Finalists

L. to R.: mgr. Rosio Gonzales, Ginny Freshley, Shondra Gray, Michelle Jones, Kim Dowden, 2nd Row, L. to R.: Michelle Hall, Lorenda Smartt, Shelia Ford, Karen Majaras, Ellen Glossup, Michelle Hall, Kneeling: Ronnakee Woods, Angie Appleby, Shannon Beck.

Girls' Record: 9-5

1986

Boys' Record: 16-13

Front: Julia Trevino, Tonya Thomas, Yvette Borrero, Carolyn West. Back Row: Angela Appley, Melinda Burnette, Maxine Wright, Kim Dowden, Chandra Gray, Michele Jones, Ginny Freshley, Angela Thomas, Karen Howard, Ronneeke Woods.

Girls' Record: 6-15

1987

LHS Varsity Basketball Team

Boys' Record: 20-7

LHS Girls Varsity Basketball Team

Girls' Record: 15-15

1988

Rebels' Ray Washington eyes the basket as Cats' Andrew Mahlett eyes the ball.
Michael Meeks — Staff photographer

Boys' Record: 17-16

Girls' Record: 17-10

1989

Boys' Record 27-9, State Semi-Finalists

Girls' Record: 18-10

1990

Boys' Record: 27-7

Girls' Record: 10-18

1991

Boys' Record: 25-10, District Champions

Girls' Record 25-7; Quarterfinalists, District Champions

<u>1992</u>

Boys' Record: 21-11

Girls' Record: 20-8. Tied for District Title

1993

Ennis Flowers — Leesville

Leesville bows out

DeRIDDER—For the Leesville Wampus Cats Saturday night it was a case of so near yet so far in their bid to gain second place in the District 3-5A race against LaGrange, but the Gators came away with the 58-55 overtime victory.

The game was close most of the way.

LaGrange jumped out to an early 17-13 lead at the end of the first quarter, and held a 26-22 advantage at the half.

Ronnie DeGray scored the first points of the third quarter, to cut the LaGrange lead to 26-24, but LaGrange countered to improve to 28-24.

LaGrange pulled out to a 37-26 lead later in the third quarter, but the Wampus Cats had closed the gap to tie the score at 38-38 with 47 seconds remaining in the quarter on Michael Cole's field goal.

Demond Mallet put the Wampus Cats ahead by a 40-38 margin at the end of the quarter.

In the final quarter, the Wampus Cats pulled out to a 42-38 lead on Ennis Flowers field goal, but LaGrange countered with four points to tie the score at 42-42.

Leesville pulled ahead 46-42 on field goals by Flowers and Mallet, but LaGrange came back to tie it at 46-46 with five minutes remaining in regulation.

LaGrange pulled ahead 49-46 when Earnie Jackson hit a pair of free-throws with 3:52 remaining in regulation, and Leesville got within one at 49-48 on a free-throw by Keith Pittman with 1:07 remaining.

Mark White hit the field goal which sent the game into overtime at 50-50. Pittman had a chance to win the game with four seconds left but his shot bounced off the rim.

In the overtime period, LaGrange jumped ahead 52-50 on a field goal by Tavaris White, but Cole countered to tie the score at 52-52.

LaGrange went ahead 54-52 on a pair of free-throws with 1:23 remaining.

The Wampus Cats chances of making the playoffs died with the loss.

Boys' Record 20-10

Leesville 40, West Monroe 34 — Mary McCrystal scored 10 points to lead Leesville past West Monroe in the first round of the Class 5A state playoffs.

Leesville, 20-11 and a wildcard from District 3-5A, will travel to face Byrd, a 60-32 winner over LaGrange, Monday night.

West Monroe, which finishes its season at 24-10, was paced by Katoya Scott with a game-high 13.

Girls' Record 20-12

1994

Boys' Record: 25-8, District Champions

Girls' Record: 13-15

1995

Boys' Record: 21-10, District Champions

Bottom Row Amy Martin, Manager, Cordelia Miller, Nikki Hiers, Eula Hickman, Nya Wilson, Tracey Herzog, Manager. Middle Row Tina Holland, Angela Davidson, Cornelia Miller, Amanda Taplin. Top Row Tori Daniel, Matricia Keys, Manager Emily McDonald.

Girls' Record: 20-12, District Champions

1996

Boys' Record: 27-8, State Runner Up, District Champions

Girls' Record: 17-12, District Champions

1997

Wampus Cat Basketball

Front row: Kedric Green, Rod Gates, Tee Jackson, James Brown, Dustin Smith, Derrick Wright.
Back row: Brian Holt, J.J. Joiner, Ron McCray, Darnell Bradley, Quinton Buchanan, Jamal Wilson, Dave Bailey, Clint Skinner.

Boys' Record: 25-9, District Champions

Lady Cats Basketball

Lady Cats Varsity

Girls' Record: 19-9, District Champions

1998

1998 4-4A All-District Boys basketball team

FIRST TEAM

J.J. Joiner, Leesville	6-0	Sr	19.5
Harry Frank, Eunice	6-8	Sr	15.0
Ryan Temple, DeRidder	6-4	Sr	19.8
Walter Sampson, Crowley	6-3	Sr	25.0
Jeff Brown, Leesville	5-10	Sr	18.1

SECOND TEAM

Charles Anderson, Eunice	5-6	So	15.0
James Greening, DeRidder	6-4	Sr	15.4
David Carpenter, Sam Houston	6-8	So	13.8
Larry Ashworth, DeRidder	5-10	Sr	14.6
Derrick Wright, Leesville	5-11	Jr	16.2

MOST VALUABLE PLAYER
J.J. Joiner, Leesville
COACH OF THE YEAR
Robert Trent, Eunice
DEFENSIVE PLAYER OF THE YEAR
Harry Frank, Eunice

1997-98 LSWA Class 4A All-State Basketball Team

Boys' First Team

Player	School	Ht.	Class	PPG
Ernest Dixon	Ellender	6-4	Jr.	18.0
Brandon Dickerson	Woodlawn	6-3	Jr.	18.2
Derrick Zimmerman	Wossman	6-2	Jr.	22.2
Thomas Davis	Pineville	6-8	Jr.	20.9
Brandon Mouton	St. Thomas More	6-4	Soph.	18.6

Boys' Second Team

Player	School	Ht.	Class	PPG
Kaseby Williams	Peabody	6-0	Sr.	14.1
Mark Schwab	St. Paul's	6-10	Sr.	22.0
J.J. Joiner	Leesville	6-0	Sr.	19.5
Harry Frank	Eunice	6-8	Sr.	15.0
Fred Marshall	Carver	6-2	Sr.	21.5

Boys' Record: 21-8, District Champions, Tied

1998 4-4A All-District Girls basketball team

FIRST TEAM

Hope Sinclair, Crowley	5-7	Sr.	18.0
Shanel Handy, DeRidder	5-4	Jr.	19.5
Deidre Williams, DeRidder	5-7	Sr.	16.6
Angela Davidson, Leesville	6-2	Sr.	22.0
Melanie Vidrine, Sam Houston	5-9	Sr.	15.6

SECOND TEAM

Crystal Carmouche, Crowley	5-9	Jr.	13.4
Nevia Marks, DeRidder	5-10	Sr.	14.5
Laricia Poullard, Eunice	5-6	So.	14.0
Viola Thomas, Leesville	5-10	Jr.	11.3
Brooke Hebert, Sam Houston	5-9	Sr.	10.1

MOST VALUABLE PLAYER
Angela Davidson, Leesville
COACH OF THE YEAR
Stacy Hughes, DeRidder

Girls' First Team

Player	School	Ht.	Class	PPG
Kisha James	Pineville	5-6	Sr.	33.0
Angela Davidson	Leesville	5-11	Sr.	22.0
Shondra Johnson	St. Mary's	5-9	Sr.	30.9
Jamie Thomatis	Ursuline	5-11	Sr.	27.6
Selena Businelle	Assumption	6-1	Sr.	15.6

Girls' Second Team

Player	School	Ht.	Class	PPG
Charlotte Green	St. Thomas More	5-7	Jr.	18.0
Samantha Alston	Wossman	5-8	Jr.	16.0
Jennifer Edwards	Northwood	5-9	Sr.	16.5
Roneeka Hodges	O.P. Walker	5-9	Soph.	21.3
Jayme Chikos	Bishop Sullivan	5-8	Jr.	17.5

Girls' Record: 17-11, District Champions

1999

Boys' Record: 24-7

Row 1: Tiffany Hudgens, Kristi Massey, Sarah Teal, Ebony Parker. Row 2: Seini Tonga, Natasha Johnson, Latasha Lewis, Viola Thomas, Sheronda Bowers, Sepi Tonga.

Girls' Record: 22-7 District Champions

2000

Boys' Record: 33-5. State Runner-up, District Champions

Varsity: 1st row: #12 Erin Smith, #30 Jennifer Neuman, #24 Krystal Massey, #32 Summer Sexson, #21 Tiffany Hudgens; 2nd row: #34 Jennifer Butler, #54 Ebony Parker, #53 Aviva Woods, #42 Natasha Johnson, #40 Sheronda Bowers, #45 Shalasha Lorne

Girls' Record: 14-14

2001

Boys' Record: 28-8, State Champions, District Champions

Girls' Record: 20-13, District Champions

2002

Marcus Singleton, Cordell Upshaw, Eric Woods, Onterio Agnew, Aaron Moore
Darius Adams, JoJuan Cranson, Darryl Joiner, Michael Davis, Chris Elkins, Jermaine Gwinn

Boys' Record: 20-10

Jessica Foster, Ashley Mitchell, Ashley Landrum, Christie Potter, Nicole Saverino, Jessica Bustard, Courtney Cavanaugh, Aviance McClauren, Sarah Armstrong, Tasha Goble, Allison Willing, Lesley Poteat, Jessica Safoa, Brooklyn Roberts, Jessica Cavanaugh, Heather Summers

Girls' Record: 17-10

2003

Wampus Cats rip Bobcats

BY JOHN BURSON
Sports Writer

LEESVILLE – The Eunice High Bobcats proved to be no match for the Leesville High Wampus Cats here Friday night as the Wampus Cats topped the Bobcats by an 85-61 margin.

Leesville jumped to a 23-16 lead after the end of the first quarter, but the Bobcats cut the lead to 40-35 by the half. It was all Wampus Cats, however, in the third quarter as they outscored the Bobcats 24-12 to take control of the contest.

The loss dropped the Bobcats to 0-5 in district play and to 9-14 overall.

The leading scorer for the Bobcats was Josh Neville with 19 points. Neville hit seven field goals and was good on five of nine free throws.

Lee Edwards added 18 points for the Cats. Edwards hit three three-point goals. Ike Rhines also hit the double-figure mark with 10 points. Other scorers for the Bobcats included Harry Coward and Gaston Woods, with four apiece; and Josh Watley, Thaddeus Godfrey, and Colby Lemelle, with two apiece.

Donte Sweat led Leesville with 20 points. Sweat hit seven field goals, including one three-point effort, and five of five free throws.

Darryl Joiner added 18 and Frank Lary had 16 for the Wampus Cats. Derrious Adams chipped in with 11 points.

Boys' Record: 19-11

GIRLS
First Team
Shan Moore, Minden,	5-10, Sr, 20.7
Sasha Stadium, Ellender,	5-9, So, 16.0
Taryn Achord, Walker,	5-10, Sr, 17.1
Voneshia Williams, Bolton,	5-11, Jr, 18.5
Khalilah Mitchell, St. Marys,	5-11, Sr, 19.2

Second Team
Tylnn Henderson, Assumption,	5-0, Jr, 14.0
Tiffany Thomas, McKinley,	5-10, Sr, 21.6
Shonte Kennedy, Leesville,	5-6, So, 22.0
Neosho Meadows, Woodlawn,	5-7, Jr, 9.0
Sally Padgett, St. Thomas More,	6-0, Sr, 15.5

Girls' Record: 12-16

2004

DISTRICT 3-4A

Boys
First Team

John Ford	Peabody	G	Sr.
Terrance Blake	**Leesville**	**G**	**Jr.**
Ken Baker	Peabody	G	Sr.
Lance Brasher	Peabody	F	Sr.
DeAndre Eggins	Peabody	F	Jr.
Demar Dotson	Alexandria	C	Sr.

Second Team

Doug Washington	Pineville	G	Sr.
Lem Lyons	Pineville	G	Jr.
Frank Larry	**Leesville**	**F**	**So.**
Fred Anderson	Tioga	C	Sr.

Most Valuable Player – John Ford, Peabody
Coach of the Year – Charles Smith, Peabody

Boys' Record: 23-11

Girls
First Team

Shonté Kennedy	**Leesville**	**G**	**Jr.**
Jasmine Eli	Peabody	G	Sr.
Jessica Hornage	Peabody	F	Sr.
Courtney Carter	**Leesville**	**F**	**Jr.**
Emily Palermo	Pineville	F	So.

Second Team

Jennifer Blake	**Leesville**	**G**	**So.**
LaShondra Swafford	Tioga	F	So.
Tasha Freeman	Bolton	F	Sr.
Kelli Brasher	Peabody	C	Jr.
Voneshia Williams	Bolton	C	Sr.

Most Valuable Player – Jasmine Eli, Peabody
Coach of the Year – Greg Knox, Peabody

Leesville's Courtney Carter soars over defenders in the 66-40 win over Class 3A Marksville on Tuesday night.

Girls' Record 20-11 GET A NEW PICTURE

2005

Boys' Record: 27-8

Girls' Record: 26-6

2006

DISTRICT 3-4A
Boys
First Team
Dominic Knight, ASH, Jr., 14.1
Larry Frank, LHA, Sr., 20.5
Rodney Jones, PMHS, Sr., 25.0
Marcus Simmons, PMHS, Jr., 16.0
Charles Clark, THS, Jr., 16.0

Boys Record: 12-14

Girls
First Team
Kayla Guidry, Peabody, Sr., 15.0
Emily palermo, Pineville, Sr., 15.0
LaShonda Swafford, Tioga, Sr., 11.0
Jennifer Blake, Leesville, Sr., 15.0
Keri Thomas, Peabody, Fr., 12.0

Girls' Record: 10-15

2007

3-4A
First Team
Marcus Simmons, Peabody, Sr.
Raphelle "Rudy" Turner, Peabody, Sr.
Charles Clark, Tioga, Sr.
Carlos Tatum, Tioga, Sr.
Marcus Rim, Leesville, Sr.

Second Team
Desmond King, Peabody, Jr.
Jonathan Roque, ASH, Sr.
Mel Smith, Tioga, Sr.
William McNeill, Peabody, Jr.
Dontae Cannon, ASH, So.

Honorable Mention
Deon Williams, ASH
Robert Harrington, Leesville
Darren Cloud, Pineville
Shelton Burns, Pineville
Kevin Joiner, Pineville
Austen Baker, Peabody
Derrick Howard, Peabody
Travis Augustine, Tioga

LEESVILLE 53, PINEVILLE 45

Eric Shepherd scored 15 points to lead Leesville to a District 3-4A win over the Rebels. After struggling to score a combined 10 points over the second and third quarters, Pineville exploded for 24 points in the final period. However, the Rebels couldn't contain Leesville enough for the comeback.

Shelton Burns scored 13 points to lead Pineville, which fell to 14-10, 1-4 in 3-4A. Marcus Rim contributed 11 points for the Wampus Cats, who improved to 16-11, 2-3.

Boys' Record: 16-12

NO PICTURES FOUND

Girls' Record: 11-16

2008

Top left to right Coach Rodney wells . Players Phillip Edwards, Demetrius Mark, Ezell Craft, Tracy Smith, Kevin Edwards Dionte Kennedy Coach Tracy Reese
Bottom row players Christopher Lewis, Steve White, Levander Liggins, Marcus Palmer, Norman Allen

Boys' Record: 17-18

District 3-4A
First Team
Alonda Williams, Peabody, Sr.
Shambrica Chatman, Peabody, Sr.
Karensa Ellis, ASH, Jr.
Shemekia Jones, Grant, Sr.
Aeriona Ray, Tioga, So.
Second Team
Cara Miley, Tioga, Fr.
Tiffany Wallace, Leesville, Fr.
Alyse Lacking, Leesville, Sr.
Chrishonda Whitlock, Peabody, So.
Allison Evans, ASH, Jr.
Hannah Jeffress, Grant, Sr.
Most Valuable Player: Alonda Williams, Peabody
Coach of the Year: Carol Elder, ASH

Girls' Record 4-24

2009

Wampus Cats top Tioga

Leesville..............................62
Tioga..................................58

TIOGA — The Leesville Wampus Cats held off a late run from the Tioga Indians to pick up a 62-58 win in a huge District 3-4A contest.

Leesville improved to 17-14 overall, 2-4 in district play with the win as the Cats prepare to entertain Alexandria on Friday.

The Cats got off to a hot start leading 18-9 at the end of the first quarter. By the halftime intermission Leesville owned a 27-15 advantage.

The Indians began to come to life offensively in the second half, using a 19-17 edge in the third to trim the deficit to 10 points entering the fourth quarter, 44-34.

Tioga outscored Leesville, 24-18, in the fourth, but it wasn't enough to stop the Cats from getting the win.

Levander Liggins scored 25 points to pace the Cats, while Dominique Woods and Anthony Davis came in with 11 and 10 points respectively.

Rodney Williams led all scorers with 28 points for Tioga, while Steve Simmons finished with 10 points in the loss.

Boys' Record: 17-16

District 3-4A
FIRST TEAM
Keri Thomas, Peabody
Laken Reed, Peabody
Yahtesha Bradley, Tioga
Tiffany Wallace, Leesville
Kymeshia Smith, ASH
SECOND TEAM
Karensa Ellis, ASH
Chrishonda Whitlock, Peabody
Darrecia Evans, ASH
Chelsey Martin, Leesville
Erin McCain, Grant
MVP: Keri Thomas, Peabody
Coach of the Year: Michael Burks, Peabody

Girls Record: 8-12

2010

Boys' Record: 5-19

Class 4A All-State Basketball Teams

GIRLS
FIRST TEAM

Player	School	Ht	Yr	Avg.
Liann McCarthy	Ursuline	5-10	Sr.	17.7
Shalyn Riley	Jennings	5-7	Jr.	18.4
Theresa Plaisance	Vandebilt Catholic	6-5	Sr.	16.0
KK Babin	St. Michael	5-5	Sr.	15.7
Blessin Bush	Glen Oaks	5-10	Sr.	17.0

SECOND TEAM

Player	School	Ht	Yr	Avg.
Lulu Perry	Benton	5-6	So.	25.5
Tiffany Wallace	**Leesville**	**5-9**	**Jr.**	**29.0**
Chelsea Broussard	Beau Chene	6-0	Sr.	17.0
Natasha Wiltz	Cecilia	5-8	Sr.	24.5
Sharnice Brooks	Bastrop	6-0	Jr.	15.0

Girls' Record: 18-14

2011

Boys' Record: 17-16

Girls' Record: 20-7

2012

Boys' Record: 17-12

Girls' Record: 9-14

2013

Boys' Record: 27-6

Girls' Record: 24-8

2014

Boys' Record: 17-14

Girls' Record: 3-14

2015

Boys' Record: 24-8

Girls' Record: 16-8

2016

Boys' Record: 21-14

Girls' Record: 3-15

2017

DISTRICT 3-4A
FIRST TEAM

	Ht	Cl	Avg
Chris Osten, Crowley	6-8	Sr	11.8
Randy Gladney, DeRidder	6-8	Jr	15.1
J'Son Brooks, LaGrange	6-6	Sr	12.4
DaVantre Vitor, W-Marion	5-10	Sr	15.6
Ferontay Banks, W-Marion	6-6	Sr	17.3

MOST VALUABLE PLAYER
DaVantre Vitor, Washington-Marion
COACH OF THE YEAR
Albert Hartwell, Washington-Marion

SECOND TEAM

	Ht	Cl	Avg
Terrell Lucas, Leesville	6-1	Sr	12.2
Drekylon Gibson, Rayne	5-10	Jr	12.0
Dre Bagley, DeRidder	6-0	Jr	13.7
Josh Burnett, Crowley	5-9	Jr	13.3
Michael Thomas, W-Marion	6-1	Jr	12.3

ALL-DEFENSIVE TEAM
Perry Myles, Crowley; Deirico Smith, DeRidder; Donte' Clark, LaGrange; Kydedrion Spriggs, Leesville; Dontray Leopold, Rayne; Diallo Small, W-Marion.
HONORABLE MENTION
Marcus Landry, LaGrange; Cody Stansberry, W-Marion; Joseph Davis, DeRidder; Deirico Smith, DeRidder.

Boys' Record: 11-21

Girls' Record: 9-18

2018

Boys' Record: 20-12

Girls' Record: 19-14

2019

Boys' Record: 32-4, State Semi-Finalist (Final 4), District Champions

Girls' Record: 12-18

2020

Boys' Record: 13-18

Girls' Record: 2-27

2021

Boys' Record: 6-16

Girls' Record: 2-16

2022

Boys' Record: 7-15

Girls' Record: 12-13

2023

Boys' Record: 8-23

Girls' Record: 18-12

2024

Boys' Record: 13-16

Girls' Record: 21-11

Scrapbook Pages

Photos, Results, Box Scores, All-District Selections & other Memories

Jeremiah Lee 2024

JU'LIUN CULBERT 1st Team All-District

Shyann McCummings 2023

Amaya Thomas, 2022

Carlos Pagan 2020

2019. Trip to the Semi-Finals

2018

2015 Dashawn Lewis

2017 Terrell Lucas

2014

DISTRICT 3-4A BOYS — 2016
FIRST TEAM

Player, School	Ht	CL	Avg
Jacq'co Price, Crowley	6-2	Sr	11.9
Randy Gladney, DeRidder	6-7	Soph	14.3
J'Son Brooks, LaGrange	6-6	Jr	18.6
Derrick Brock, Leesville	6-0	Sr	15.4
Christian Edwards, W-Marion	6-5	Jr	14.3

DISTRICT 3-4A GIRLS — 2016
FIRST TEAM

Player, School	CL
Charlesha Dugas, Rayne	Sr
Whitley Larry, Rayne	Sr
Delaisha Thomas, Lagrange	Jr
Keke Culbert, Leesville	Sr
Tydianna Syas, Washington-Marion	Jr

2014 Brady Westerchil

2014

LHS 59 Peabody 45

Leesville	11	10	11	13	— 59
Peabody	14	16	17	12	— 45

Leesville (14-12, 4-7): Derrick Brock 11, Vidall Corbin 10, Donae Dias 10, Cleveland Evans 4, Keyuon Alexander 4, Darren McQueen 3, Jatorrey Smith 3. Peabody (21-4, 3-1): Gabriel Jordan 18, Robert Guillette 12, Cedric Russell 11, Jeff Sibley 6, Jacoby Ross 6, Danmon O'Conner 6.

2014

Boys: Minden downs Airline; Benton rallies past Lakeside

2013 Darren McQueen ties Gary McDonald's single game scoring record from 1970

2012

2012

CLASS 4A
Bi-District Results
Wash.-Marion at Warren Easton
Broadmoor 46, Ellender 42
Alexandria 57, Wossman 34
Helen Cox 73, Franklin Parish 29
STM 82, Peabody 40
Gabriel 45, Bastrop 42
Leesville 81, Belaire 75
Neville 32, Benton 17

2013 Girls' Playoffs

Chelsea Martin,
All-State 2011

2011 Diontay Thurman and Vidal Corbin

Levander Liggins

Class 4A All-State Basketball Teams

GIRLS
FIRST TEAM

Player	School	Ht	Yr	Avg.
Liann McCarthy	Ursuline	5-10	Sr.	17.7
Shalyn Riley	Jennings	5-7	Jr.	18.4
Theresa Plaisance	Vandebilt Catholic	6-5	Sr.	16.0
KK Babin	St. Michael	5-5	Sr.	15.7
Blessin Bush	Glen Oaks	5-10	Sr.	17.0

SECOND TEAM

Player	School	Ht	Yr	Avg.
Lulu Perry	Benton	5-6	So.	25.5
Tiffany Wallace	Leesville	5-9	Jr.	29.0
Chelsea Broussard	Beau Chene	6-0	Sr.	
N. Wiltz	Cecilia	5-8	Sr.	
Sh. Brooks	Bastrop	6-0	Jr.	

Outstanding Player
Theresa Plaisance, Vandebilt Catholic
Coach of the Year
Melanie Durio, Beau Chene

2010: Most Points Per Game in LHS Girls' Basketball History

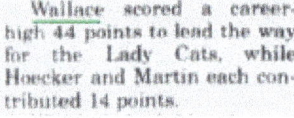

Wallace scored a career-high 44 points to lead the way for the Lady Cats, while Hoecker and Martin each contributed 14 points.

Tiffany Wallace scores 44 vs Peabody in 2010

District 3-4A — 2009
FIRST TEAM
Markel Brown, Peabody
Dontae Cannon, ASH
Ricardo Brown, Grant
Levander Liggins, Leesville
Troy Jones, Peabody
Rodney Williams, Tioga
SECOND TEAM
Corey Brown, Grant
Phillip Mathews, ASH
Josh Ivory, Peabody
Hakeem Welch, ASH
Michael Ford, Peabody
MVP: Markel Brown, Peabody
Coach of the Year: Charles Smith, Peabody
Honorable Mention: Ked Lair, Tioga; Antonio Davis, Grant; Demetrius Mark, Leesville; Zack Bush, Grant; Deonte Riser, AS...

District 3-4A — 2009
FIRST TEAM
Keri Thomas, Peabody
Lakan Reed, Peabody
Yahtesha Bradley, Tioga
Tiffany Wallace, Leesville
Kymeshia Smith, ASH
SECOND TEAM
Karensa Ellis, ASH
Chrishonda Whitlock, Peabody
Darrecia Evans, ASH
Chelsey Martin, Leesville
Erin McCain, Grant

3-4A All District Team — 2007

GIRLS
First Team

Name	School	Cl.
Keri Thomas	Peabody	Soph
Alonda Williams	Peabody	Jr
Courtney Barber	Tioga	Sr
Kasheaf Pinder	Tioga	Sr
Jordan Rawson	Pineville	Sr

Second Team

Shaunise Brown	Peabody	Sr
Megan Washington	Pineville	Soph
Brittany Cook	Pineville	Sr
Tyra Teasley	Pineville	Jr
Margaret Mansour	Pineville	Jr

MOST VALUABLE PLAYER: Keri Thomas, Peabody
CO-COACH OF THE YEAR: Michael Burks, Peabody
Honorable Mention: Ashley Cesear, Alexandria; Ala Johnson, Alexandria; Tremeka Ford, Leesville; Shambrica Chatman, Peabody; Chrishanda Whitlock, Peabody.

BOYS
First Team

Name	School	Cl.
Marcus Simmons	Peabody	Sr
Charles Clark	Tioga	Sr
Raphelle Turner	Peabody	Sr
Marcus Sim	Leesville	Sn
Carlos Tatum	Tioga	Sr

Second Team

Desmond King	Peabody	NG
Jonathan Rogue	Alexandria	NG
Mel Smith	Tioga	NG
William McNeil	Peabody	NG
Dontae Cannon	Alexandria	NG

MOST VALUABLE PLAYER: Marcus Simmons, Peabody
Honorable Mention: Caron Williams, Alexandria; Robert Herrington, Leesville; Darren Cloud, Pineville; Shelton Burns, Pineville; Kem Joiner, Pineville; Austen Baker, Peabody; Derrick Howard, Peabody; Travis Augustine, Tioga.

District 3-4A — 2008
First Team
Desmond King, Peabody, Sr.
Bobo Brown, Grant, Sr.
Dontae Cannon, ASH, Jr.
Mychal Horn, Peabody, Sr.
William McNeill, Peabody, Sr.
Second Team
Corey Blake, ASH, Sr.
Doc Welch, Tioga, So.
Markel Brown, Peabody, So.
Ricardo Brown, Grant, Jr.
Dionte Kennedy, Leesville, Sr.
Honorable Mention
ASH: Philip Matthews, Randon Holly; Grant: Jordan Spencer, Corey Brown, Zack ...ille: Norman Allen; Peabody; ...Tioga: Corey Alexander, Ber-
...Player: Desmond King,
...Year: Charles Smith, Peabody

District 3-4A — 2008
First Team
Alonda Williams, Peabody, Sr.
Shambrica Chatman, Peabody, Sr.
Karensa Ellis, ASH, Jr.
Shemekia Jones, Grant, Sr.
Aeriona Ray, Tioga, So.
Second Team
Cara Miley, Tioga, Fr.
Tiffany Wallace, Leesville, Fr.
Alyse Lacking, Leesville, Sr.
Chrishonda Whitlock, Peabody, So.
Allison Evans, ASH, Jr.

2006 — John Keyes

Joe Sowells
213 Wins

2004 — Shonte' Kennedy

2005 — Malcom Selma

Daryl Joiner

2003

2002

Eric Woods

GIRLS 2003
First Team
Shan Moore, Minden,	5-10, Sr, 20.7
Sasha Stadium, Ellender,	5-9, So, 16.0
Taryn Achord, Walker,	5-10, Sr, 17.1
Voneshia Williams, Bolton,	5-11, Jr, 18.5
Khailah Mitchell, St. Marys,	5-11, Sr, 19.2

Second Team
Tyinn Henderson, Assumption,	5-0, Jr, 14.0
Tiffany Thomas, McKinley,	5-10, Sr, 21.6
Shonte Kennedy, Leesville,	5-6, So, 22.0
Neosho Meadows, Woodlawn,	5-7, Jr, 9.0
Sally Padgett, St. Thomas More,	6-0, Sr, 15.5

Prep Basketball
2001-2002 CLASS 4A All-STATE BASKETBALL TEAMS

BOYS
First Team
Name, School	Ht	Cl	Avg
Darrel Mitchell Jr., St. Martinville	5-11	Sr	24.6
Chris Phillips, Washington-Marion	6-3	Sr	17.7
Tristan King, Peabody	6-4	Sr	18.4
Brandon Bass, Capitol	6-6	Jr	18.0
Ricky Woods, Carver	6-4	Sr	18.6

Second Team
Eric Woods, Leesville	6-4	Sr	17.0
Burnell Johnson, Ellender	6-5	Jr	17.0
Jontae Turpin, Neville	5-7	Jr	7.5
Jessie Luce, Pineville	6-5	Sr	17.4
Tyrone Hamilton, B.T. Washington	5-10	So	17.5

MOST VALUABLE PLAYER
Darrel Mitchell Jr., St. Martinville
COACH OF THE YEAR
Mack Guillory, Washington-Marion

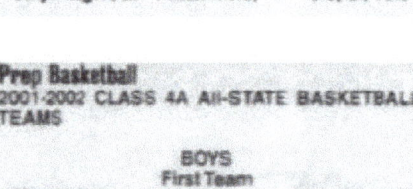

Sheronda Bowers 2001

Derrious Adams 2002

Leesville coach Grant Westerchil watches the action Saturday night as the Wampus Cats play the Woodlawn Panthers. Leesville beat Woodlawn for the school's first basketball title and only the second state title in school history. Westerchil, the Wampus Cats coach for the past seven years, announced his resignation in the post-game press conference.

4-4A All-District girls — 2001

FIRST TEAM
Name, school	Cl.	Ht.	Avg.
Sheronda Bowers, Leesville	Sr	5-8	26.0
Samantha Ford, Sam Houston	Jr	5-6	12.6
Cedrina Charles, DeRidder	Jr	5-6	18.0
Cassidy Jones, Crowley	So	5-9	20.0
Amber Jenkins, Wash-Marion	Sr	5-11	13.0

SECOND TEAM
Name, school	Cl.	Ht.	Avg.
Ebony Parker, Leesville	Sr	5-6	10.0
Natasha Johnson, Leesville	Sr	6-1	9.0
Tene Matthews, Wash-Marion	So	5-7	9.0
Ashley Smith, Wash-Marion	Sr	6-0	9.0
Rebecca Lund, DeRidder	Jr	5-7	11.0

MOST VALUABLE PLAYER
Sheronda Bowers, Leesville
COACH OF THE YEAR
Joe Sowell, Leesville

4-4A All-District boys — 2001

FIRST TEAM
Name, school	Cl.	Ht.	Avg.
Josh Thibodeaux, Eunice	Sr	6-2	29.5
Eric Woods, Leesville	Jr	6-3	21.0
Anthony Johnson, Wash-Marion	Sr	6-2	13.6
Chris Campbell, Leesville	Sr	6-2	17.0
Andre Herron, DeRidder	Sr	6-0	14.3

Second Team
Name, school	Cl.	Ht.	Avg.
Jeff Jones, DeRidder	Sr	6-3	17.4
Marcus Johnson, Leesville	Jr	6-2	14.5
Bryce DeJean, Crowley	Jr	6-1	14.4
Chris Phillips, Wash-Marion	Jr	6-3	12.5
Kyle Savant, Eunice	Sr	6-3	10.0

MOST VALUABLE PLAYER
Josh Thibodeaux, Eunice
COACH OF THE YEAR
Grant Westerchil, Leesville

Chris Campbell — 2001

Ebony Parker — 2000
Kedric Green — 1999

ALL-STATE BASKETBALL — CLASS 4A — 2000

BOYS
First Team
Player, Team	Ht	Cl	Av
Darnell Bradley, Leesville	6-5	Sr.	19.8
Reggie Rambo, Peabody	6-6	Sr.	18.6
Rashid Smith, Peabody	6-3	Sr.	16.5
Brandon Mouton, S.T. More	6-5	Sr.	23.1
Chris Duhon, Salmen	6-4	Sr.	23.0

Second Team
Player, Team	Ht	Cl	Av
Cedric Davis, Many	6-2	Jr.	20.4
Bryan Rusley, Parkway	6-1	Jr.	18.9
Josh Thibodeaux, Eunice	6-1	Jr.	31.6
Darrel Mitchell, St. Martinville	5-10	So.	22.2
Wand Steward, Ellender	5-10	Sr.	23.4
Leon Vaal, Vandebilt	6-3	Sr.	22.6

Outstanding Player: Chris Duhon, Salmen.
Coach of the Year: Grant Westerchil, Leesville

Leesville 78, Bishop Sullivan 38

Bishop Sullivan	8	7	8	15	—38
Leesville	23	25	21	9	—78

Bishop Sullivan (10-13)
Chad Guzzarno 3, Jason Fernandez 14, Ben Buttita 2, Keith Norris 2, Jonathan Stewart 9, Jeff Hough 8.

Leesville (24-6)
Derrick Wright 21, Darnell Bradley 12, Macklin McCray 15, Tee Jackson 5, Tyrone Parker 18, Chris Campbell 6, Lamont Ball 1.

1998-99 District 4-4A Girls' All-District Basketball Team

First Team
Player	School	Class	PPG
Crystal Carmouche	Crowley	Sr.	18.0
Shanel Handy	DeRidder	Sr.	21.5
Sheronda Bowers	Leesville	Soph.	18.0
Viola Thomas	Leesville	Sr.	11.0
Tiffany Brown	Sam Houston	Sr.	12.0

Second Team
Player	School	Class	PPG
Tiffany Boudreaux	Crowley	Sr.	11.2
LaRicia Poullard	Eunice	Jr.	12.3
Jenett Bearby	DeRidder	Sr.	10.3
Sepi Tonga	Leesville	Sr.	11.0
Christy Daniels	Sam Houston	Sr.	9.0

Most Valuable Player: Crystal Carmouche, Crowley.
Coach of the Year: Joe Sowells, Leesville.

1997-98 Class 4A All-State Basketball Teams

Player of the Year: Thomas Davis, Pineville
Coach of the Year: Kenny Almond, Woodlawn

First Team

Name	School	Cl.	Ht.	Avg.
Ernest Nixon	Ellender	Jr.	6-4	18.0
Brandon Dickerson	Woodlawn	Jr.	6-3	18.2
Derrick Zimmerman	Wossman	Jr.	6-2	22.2
Thomas Davis	Pineville	Jr.	6-8	20.6
Brandon Mouton	STM	So.	6-4	18.6

Second Team

Name	School	Cl.	Ht.	Avg.
Kaseby Williams	Peabody	Sr.	6-0	14.1
Mark Schwabs	St. Paul's	Sr.	6-10	22.0
J.J. Joiner	Leesville	Sr.	6-0	19.5
Harry Frank	Eunice	Sr.	6-8	15.0
Fred Marshall	Carver	Sr.	6-2	21.5

Leesville 65, BTW 55

Booker T. Washington	19	11	15	10	55
Leesville	14	10	17	24	65

Booker T. Washington (24-11)
Takeo Grant 2, Talia Jefferson 8, Katrina Carter 2, Kim Weaver 6, Cherise Sims 17, Tylesha Robertson 11, Chaka Jackson 9.

Leesville (17-10)
Ericka Coley 8, Sepi Tonga 2, Sheronda Bowers 9, Angela Davidson 35, Viola Thomas 11.

1998 Girls' Playoff Win

1997 Dist Title Clinched

The Leesville girls clinched the District 4-4A title with a 55-32 victory over Washington-Marion.

Leesville led 22-18 at halftime, but a 13-2 run increased that margin to 35-20.

The Lady Indians pulled within 38-28, but an 8-0 run, capped by Angela Davidson's basket with 4:05 left in the game, put Leesville up 46-28.

The Wampus Cats outrebounded Washington-Marion 47-28.

Davidson led Leesville, 18-9 and 8-1, with 18 points, followed by Viola Thomas with 10. Sonya Williams led Washington-Marion, 11-13 and 5-4, with eight points.

"I just told the girls to take care of business and take it to them and we'll be OK," said Leesville coach Joe Sowells. "We overcame a mental block in our mind because Washington-Marion had beat us down there and had beaten us the last three or four times we played them. Once we wiped that out of our mind, we came out and played."

1997 All State — Girls

First Team

Player, School	Ht.	Cl.	Avg.
Nancy Dubuisson, Salmen	5-10	Jr.	16.0
Kisha James, Pineville	5-9	Jr.	34.0
Shondra Johnson, St. Mary's	5-9	Jr.	33.3
Meishika Bowman, Peabody	6-2	Sr.	17.0
Jennifer Edwards, Northwood	5-10	Jr.	17.0

Second Team

Player, School	Ht.	Cl.	Avg.
Adrian Barnes, Wossman	6-0	Sr.	21.4
Kizzy Greene, Opelousas	5-8	Sr.	16.0
Crystal Fleming, Salmen	5-8	Sr.	12.2
Angela Davidson, Leesville	5-10	Jr.	18.4
Selena Businelle, Assumption	6-1	Jr.	19.2

Most Valuable Player: Kisha James, Pineville
Coach of the Year: Rich Lane, St. Thomas More

1997 District 4-4A boys All-District basketball team

FIRST TEAM

Junios Semien, Eunice	6-0	Sr	22.0
J.J. Joiner, Leesville	6-0	Jr	18.0
Brannon Braxton, Wash.-Marion	6-3	Sr	15.0
Harry Frank, Eunice	6-8	Jr	11.0
Jamal Wilson, Leesville	6-1	Sr	16.0

SECOND TEAM

Greg Cole, Wash.-Marion	6-4	Fr	16.0
Walter Sampson, Crowley	6-3	Jr	12.0
Hunter Bertrand, DeRidder	6-0	Sr	10.0
Keith Menard, Sam Houston	6-2	Sr	17.0
John Fontenot, Wash.-Marion	6-2	Jr	14.0

MOST VALUABLE PLAYER: Junios Semien, Eunice
COACH OF THE YEAR: Robert Trent, Eunice

1997 Jamal Wilson

BOYS 1995-96 BASKETBALL CLASS 4-4A ALL STATE TEAM

1996

NAME	SCHOOL	HT.	CLASS	AVG
Demond Mallet	Leesville	6'1"	Sr.	27.4
Edwin Daniels	Cohen	6'1"	Jr.	16.0
Terrance Simmons	Haughton	6'3"	Sr.	20.6
Lionel Brown	Opelousas	6'3"	Sr.	18.4
William Howell	Woesman	6'2"	Jr.	19.0

OUTSTANDING PLAYER - Demond Mallet, Leesville
COACH OF THE YEAR - Grant Westerchil, Leesville

2ND TEAM

NAME	SCHOOL	HT.	CLASS	AVG
Charles Hayward	Peabody	6'8"	Jr.	19.5
Torrance Robinson	Tioga	6'3"	Sr.	21.0
Reggie DeGray	Leesville	6'4"	Sr.	19.0
Tyrone Logan	STM	6'4"	Sr.	18.0
Terrell Jeter	Haughton	6'4"	Sr.	21.5

HONORABLE MENTION:

1996

1995-96 Girls' District 4-4A All-District Basketball Team

First Team

Pos.	Player	School	Class	PPG	RPG	APG	SPG
G	Hope Sinclair	Crowley	Soph.	13.5	7.7	2.5	N/A
G	LaTasha Jackson	Wash.-Marion	Sr.	13.0	5.0	3.0	4.0
C	Amanda Beckett	Sam Houston	Sr.	14.0	7.0	3.0	2.0
F	Angela Davidson	Leesville	Soph.	14.0	10.0	3.8	4.5
F	Angela Karach	DeRidder	Sr.	18.7	10.0	1.2	4.0

Second Team

Pos.	Player	School	Class	PPG	RPG	APG	SPG
G	Sonja Williams	Wash.-Marion	Soph.	10.6	6.0	2.0	2.0
G	Treneshia Aaron	Wash.-Marion	Sr.	5.0	5.0	5.0	4.0
F	Kurtina Holland	Leesville	Sr.	9.5	7.2	1.1	1.1
F	Wendi Schrader	Sam Houston	Sr.	No Statistics Available			
C	Nevia Marks	DeRidder	Soph.	14.5	9.2	1.0	1.6

Most Valuable Player: LaTasha Jackson, Washington-Marion.
Coach of the Year: Lionel Thibodeaux, Washington-Marion.

Honorable Mention

Player	School	Class	PPG	RPG	APG	SPG
Sophia Johnson	Leesville	Sr.	7.4	4.0	2.3	2.7
Tanisha Mott	Crowley	Jr.	10.1	1.8	3.2	N/A
Shanel Handy	DeRidder	Fr.	8.9	1.4	2.7	4.1
Chasity Jenkins	Wash.-Marion	Sr.	10.0	7.0	1.0	2.0
Beverly Brister	Sam Houston	Sr.	No Statistics Available			

Amanda Taplin
1995

Lonnie Thomas
1995

The 'Army Brat'
Daniels signs up for a four-year hitch with LC

1995

By John Marcase
Staff reporter

Being an Army brat, the longest Tori Daniels has ever lived in one place was four years.

By signing a basketball and academic scholarship with Louisiana College Monday afternoon, Daniels may have finally found a home.

"It wasn't a hard decision after I visited and saw how nice the people were," said Daniels, a 5-foot-11 forward from Leesville. "It's almost like home. I like the people. They make you feel at home."

Daniels played her junior and senior year at Leesville after her father was transferred to Fort Polk. She averaged 12 points and 10 rebounds per game as a senior. Daniels was born in Huntsville, Ala. and the longest she has ever lived in one place was the four years spent in Fayetteville, N.C.

Unlike the Lady Wildcats past two signees, former Buckeye standout and Northeast Louisiana transfer Ashley Smith and Marksville's Kristi Small, Daniels' knowledge of LC was limited.

"I'd heard of it before, but I didn't know what it was about or what it offered," she said.

But the one thing she offers LC is quickness and rebounding strength.

"My strong suit is rebounding," said Daniels. "The most important thing on my mind is rebounding. If I score, I score."

That type of mentality was not lost on LC coach Billy Brooks.

"I think the thing that impressed me most was her attitude on the boards," he said. "A person like that believes when the ball comes off the glass, it is her responsibility to go get it.

"We were looking for someone to come in and give us help right away."

While Daniels should help the
■ Please see LC, B-2

1994

Hub Jordan
239 Wins

1994

Reggie DeGray

1994
GIRLS
First Team
Pam Lazare, Wash-Marion, 5-2, Sr., 13.0 ppg; Mary McChrystal, Leesville, Sr., 10.9 ppg; Kim Hollier, Crowley, 5-6, Sr., 14.1 ppg; Lori Franklin, Sam Houston, 5-9, Sr., 14.0 ppg; Kari Nugent, DeRidder, Sr., 11.6 ppg.
Player of the Year: Pam Lazare, Washington-Marion
Coach of the Year: Lionel Thibodeaux, Washington-Marion

Second Team
Ursula Wilridge, Wash-Marion, 5-7, Jr., 12.0 ppg; Tori Daniel, Leesville, Jr., 10.5 ppg; Michelle Corzxdale, Sam Houston, Sr., 10.0 ppg; Stacey Nelson, DeRidder, Jr., 11.6 ppg; Jessica Broussard, Wash-Marion, 5-11, Sr., 11.0 ppg.

Honorable Mention
Danielle Spicer, Sam Houston; Cornelia Miller, Leesville; Alyson Hardy, Washington-Marion; Angel Karasch, DeRidder; Tiffany Harmon, Crowley

Tracey Thomas, Larissa McRae

Tulane inks Leesville duo

1993

Tiffany Clifton and Tracey Thomas, two senior basketball players at Leesville, signed to play with Tulane in 1993.

Clifton is a 5-foot-8 forward was an all-state honorable mention selection last season when she averaged 12.4 points and six rebounds. This year, Clifton is averaging 15.7 points and 10 rebounds. She also has a 3.2 grade point average.

Thomas, a 6-foot-2 post player, averaged 11.4 points and six rebounds last season in only her second year of varsity basketball. This year, she's averaging 17.4 points and 10 rebounds. She also has a 3.2 GPA.

1993

Ronnie DeGray

Roy Falero

1992

Tiffany Clifton

Leesville advances to regional round

The Leesville Wampus Cats advanced to the regional round of the Class AAAA state playoffs with a 74-55 victory over Lafayette Northside Friday night at Pickering.

1991

Class AAAA All-State Team

1991

BOYS
FIRST TEAM
Paul Marshall, Southwood	6-2	Sr	31.1
Duane Spencer, Cohen	6-9	Jr	27.4
Pointer Williams, St. Aug	6-0	Sr	14.4
Scotty Thurmond, Ruston	6-4	Jr	27.5
Chris Dunnington, S-wood	6-4	Jr	27.5

SECOND TEAM
Preston Coleman, Capitol	6-0	Jr	29.0
Patrick Savoy, Thibodaux	6-8	Sr	22.0
Chris Gobert, Northside	6-3	Sr	23.9
Pat Kennedy, Leesville	6-0	Sr	25.2
Richard Batiste, New Iberia	6-5	Jr	19.7

Second round scores

Second round results, through Monday night, from the Louisiana girls' high school basketball playoffs.

CLASS AAAA — 1991
BTW Shreveport 55, Byrd 50
Leesville 41, E. Ascension 39
Glen Oaks 56, C. Lafourche 42
McDonogh (35) 61, Assumption 43
Green Oaks 59, LaGrange 39
Franklin 65, Denham Springs 59, OT
S. Lafourche 57, BTW-New Orleans 48
Chalmette 40, Grace King 27

Girls Advance to Quarterfinals

District 4-AAAA

1991

First Team
Jessica Murphy, LaGrange, 5-8, jr., 14.2 ppg, 7 rpg; Tracy Fountain, Sulphur, 5-8, sr., 13 ppg, 3 apg; Candice Carnahan, Barbe, 5-8, sr., 17.1 ppg, 6.5 rpg, 79.4% FT; Karla Crockett, DeRidder, 6-1, sr., 13.6 ppg, 3 apg; Tangie Riley, Leesville, 5-3, sr., 8 ppg, 4 apg; Carissa Badger, Leesville, 5-8, sr., 11 ppg, 7 rpg.

Second Team
Mona Coleman, LaGrange, 5-5, jr., 7.2 ppg, 6.4 rpg, 6.4 apg; Becky Meyers, Sulphur, 5-9, jr., 10.3 ppg; Shyla Sicks, Barbe, 5-4, sr., 9.2 ppg, 4.4 apg; Naomi Jones, DeRidder, 5-8, jr., 13 ppg, 12 rpg; Tiffany Clifton, Leesville, 5-8, soph., 8 ppg, 6 rpg.

Honorable Mention
Geralyn Nickson, LaGrange; Katina Smith, LaGrange; Lori Deville, Sulphur; Dawn Lee, Sulphur; Jean Comeaux, Barbe; Kim Carver, Barbe; Amber Doughty, DeRidder; Courtney Doughty, DeRidder; Melanie Cottle, Leesville; Michelle Summerford, Leesville.

Outstanding Player: Carissa Badger, Leesville.
Coach of the Year: Louise Bonin, Leesville.

1990

LOUISE BONIN, HEAD COACH
ASSISTANTS — CECIL AND BOLON

Lorenzo Watkings — 1990

Stretching out

Zach White & Scott LaRue — 1991

Leesville advances to Top 24 with 73-70 victory

By Joe Durham
Leader sports editor

DeRIDDER—The Leesville Wampus Cats vaulted into the state Class AAAA tournament with a 73-70 victory over Captain Shreve Friday, but that only tells half the story.

With the Wampus Cats trailing 34-26 at the half, Patrick Kennedy came off the bench to score 16 points, mostly three-pointers, to ignite the team and send them on their way to the Top 24 in Baton Rouge this week.

The Wampus Cats will face New Orleans Shaw at 8:30 p.m. Thursday at the Pete Maravich Assembly Center on the Louisiana State University campus.

Another Wampus Cat, Neal Travis, also had the hot hand with the outside shooting. This was important, as the team from Shreveport effectively cut off the inside shooting of Robert Salisbury and David Johnson.

Neither Salisbury or Johnson finished the game in double figures.

The game was close all the way.

The score was tied twice in the first quarter at 3-3 and 5-5, before Leesville held a precarious one-point lead at the end of the first quarter 19-18.

In the second quarter, the Wampus Cats came out slowly, and Captain Shreve scored nine unanswered points to build up a 30-24 lead.

Captain Shreve led 34-26 at the halfway point.

In the third quarter, Leesville Coach Hub Jordan called on Kennedy, who promptly hit several three-pointers to pull the game close.

One three-pointer brought the Wampus Cats within one at 43-42, then Robert Salisbury countered a Captain Shreve score with a field goal to keep pace at 45-44.

Leesville went ahead 46-45 when Andre Mallet scored with 41 seconds left in the quarter, but Kennedy got the final points of the quarter at 48-47.

Captain Shreve tied the score

Leesville comes from behind, defeats Ruston

1989

AAAA girls

RUSTON — Angie Thomas and Karen Howard combined for 24 points to lead Leesville's 38-33 come-from-behind victory Thursday night over Ruston in a Class AAAA girls bi-district playoff game.

Thomas scored 14 points and had seven rebounds and Howard added 10 points for the Lady Cats, who moved to 18-9 overall and advanced to Monday night's regional playoff contest with Natchitoches-Central in Anacoco.

Ruston, which blew a 29-25 lead early in the fourth period, closed the season at 21-10. Ladondra Ethridge led Ruston with 12 points.

"We pressed and played good defense in the fourth quarter," said Leesville coach Louise Bonin. "Ruston went extremely cold and we hit the shots we had been missing."

Howard and Tangie Riley teamed to convert 5 of 6 free throws for Leesville in the game's waning moments and teammate Treva Borner had a good night on the boards, grabbing 10 rebounds in a noisy gym with few fans from Leesville.

"We had about five fans there," said Bonin, "but our kids showed a lot of class and determination."

1988
Melissa Cleary

1988
Yvette Borrero

FIRST PLAYOFF APPEARANCE SINCE 1958

Leesville 31, Barbe 29 (OT)

Barbe	9	20	22	29	29
Leesville	7	16	22	29	31

Barbe (11-11, 0-2) — Tim Cormier 2, David Burkamp 4, Chad Sarver 2, Carl Klein 14, Chad Singleton 7, Alan Logan, Mark Medlin, Bill Burkamp.

Leesville (12-9, 1-1) — Woodrow King 4, Mike Williams 3, Robert Salisbury 12, Neal Travis 2, Eric Rhodes 8, Stan Watley 2, David Johnson, Jerel Sawyer.

1988

All-State Teams

1987

average for Lafayette High. He averaged five rebounds per game. Hebert's season high was 43 points against St. Thomas More.

Cooper, a 6-foot-3 senior forward, was the MVP in District 13-AAAA after average 22.1 points for the Tigers. Cooper, a three-time All-District and two-time All-Metro pick, averaged 12.3 rebounds, 3.2 steals and 2.5 assists per game.

Eackles helped lead the Bucs to the state title with a 19.0 scoring average. The 6-4 senior forward averaged eight rebounds per game as Broadmoore went 35-3 and won its second championship in three years. Joiner, a 5-10 senior guard, hit for 25.3 points per game. He averaged five assists and shot 53 percent from the field and 76 percent from the line.

Name, School	Ht.	Cl.	Avg.
Reggie Cooper, Slidell	6-3	Sr.	22.1
Marvin Eackles, Broadmoor	6-4	Sr.	19.0
Darrell Harris, Assumption	6-6	Sr.	16.8
Joseph Hebert, Lafayette	6-3	Sr.	23.5
Dave Johnson, Morgan City	6-4	Jr.	18.1
Michael Joiner, Leesville	5-10	Sr.	25.3
John Russell, Airline	6-2	Sr.	22.2
Tim Singleton, Carver	6-2	Sr.	19.4
Kelly Small, Denham Springs	6-0	Sr.	18.2
Byron Smith, Airline	6-2	Sr.	30.5

Michael Joiner & Anthony Burns — 1987

Kim Dowden — 1987

Ginny Freshley & Angie Appleby — 1986

1985

Starting five

| Leesville | 14 | 28 | 46 | 62 |
| ASH | 16 | 31 | 50 | 58 |

Leesville (26-5) — Marro Hawkins 10, Darrell Jones 19, Darell Rush 4, Tony Marsh 19, Michael Joiner 10.

ASH (21-11) — Guy Baty 20, Daryl Scott 2, John Sampson 17, Robert Moore 6, Todd Curtis 9, Willie Bell 4, D.D. Minor 0.

Quarterfinal win Over ASH --- 1985

1984

1984
Matt Woods

1983
Connie Howard & Cynthia Faye

1983
Eric Martin

Nikita Wilson's Retired Jersey: Only one in LHS basketball history

1983

DeRidder   11 24 32 44
Leesville   11 36 63 96

DeRidder (11-13, 3-2 3-AAA) — Ronald Thomas 10, Calvin Green 8, Anthony 4, Paul Jones 8, Wayne Sims 9.

Leesville (20-2, 5-0 3-AAA) — Steve Kennedy 9, Nikita Wilson 27, Eric Martin 16, Steve Travis 4, Randy Kennedy 20, Grant Westerchill 20, Fritz Crittle 2.

Monica Boerner

1982

4-AAA All-District

District 4-AAA
FIRST TEAM

PLAYER, SCHOOL	Ht.	Class	Avg.
Kenneth Winey, Washington	5-11	Sr.	19.7
Sidney Savoy, Washington	6-4	Sr.	13.7
Kenneth Perkins, Jennings	6-1	Sr.	14.9
Gary Frank, Eunice	5-5	Sr.	13.6
Joe Banks, Westlake	5-10	Sr.	14.2

OUTSTANDING PLAYER: Kenneth Winey, Washington
OUTSTANDING COACH: Gene Duhon, Washington

SECOND TEAM
Tod Cain, Westlake; Lavon White, Leesville; Chris Carrier, Eunice; Jerome Collins, Washington; Charles Bradley, Jennings

FIRST TEAM
GIRLS

PLAYER, SCHOOL	Ht.	Class	Avg.
Julie Fruge, Jennings	5-5	Jr.	14.1
Elizabeth Cassidy, Jennings	5-8	Sr.	12.1
Regina Dixon, Leesville	5-8	Jr.	17.0
Randi Dixon, Westlake	5-9	Sr.	15.0
Imelda Goodly, Washington	5-8	Sr.	18.0

OUTSTANDING PLAYER: Julie Fruge, Jennings
OUTSTANDING COACH: Daniel Miller, Jennings

SECOND TEAM
Alberta Bradley, Jennings; Carolyn Mouton, Washington; Cheryl Duhon, Westlake; Vanessa Prater,

District 3-AAA Boys All District
FIRST TEAM

Player, School	Ht.	Class	Avg.
Nikita Wilson, Leesville	6-7	Jr.	14.0
Norbert Rosendoll, DeRidder	5-9	Sr.	14.9
Mike Lewis, West Lake	6-0	Jr.	14.0
Eddie Jones, Washington	5-11	Sr.	13.0
Marl Gray, Jennings	6-2	Sr.	15.2

SECOND TEAM
Eric Travis and Shelton Hickerson, Leesville; Patrick Kennedy, Washington; Darrell Lewis, West Lake; Alvin Johnson, Oakdale.

MOST VALUABLE PLAYER: Nikita Wilson, Leesville.
COACH OF THE YEAR: Michael Mallet, Leesville.

District 3-AAA Boys All District
FIRST TEAM

Player, School	Ht.	Class	Avg.
Treasure Thomas, DeRidder	5-10	Sr.	15.3
Julie Fruge, Jennings	5-5	Sr.	10.5
Jill Knight, Jennings	5-9	Jr.	11.4
Regina Dixon, Leesville	5-6	Sr.	17.0
Monica Boerner, Leesville	5-10	Sr.	17.0

SECOND TEAM
Cheryl Duhon, West Lake; Vanessa Prater, Oakdale; Alberta Bradley, Jennings; Julia Johnson, DeRidder; Dee Dunn, Sam Houston.

MOST VALUABLE PLAYER: Treasure Thomas, DeRidder
COACH OF THE YEAR: Danny Miller, Jennings.

1980

1980 Keith Joiner

1981 Cats' Lavon White —33 in the opener—

1976

1974-75
DISTRICT·4·AAA CHAMPS

RANDALL SMITH
JOHN JOINER
DENO BROWN
TRACY TINSLEY
DEXTER UPSHAW
LAWRENCE JOINER

UNDEFEATED

COACH:
KEITH
ANDREWS

DENNIS JOINER
RAYMOND SMITH
DENNIS MAYEAUX
SAMMY BURSH
DENNIS VAN DINE
RUSSELL MURPHY

4-3A ALL-DISTRICT FIRST TEAM

Player, School	Hgt.	Class
John Joiner, Leesville	6-2	Sr.
James Harmon, Rayne	6-3	Jr.
Cornelius Barber, Westlake	6-0	Sr.
Robert Joubert, Westlake	6-4	Jr.
Mike Ross, Jennings	6-3	Jr.

SECOND TEAM

Deno Brown, Leesville	5-10	Sr.
Randall Smith, Leesville	6-0	Sr.
Van Richmond, Westlake	6-0	Sr.
Randy Darbonne, Wash.	5-11	Soph.
Mike Granger, Eunice	6-3	Sr.

OUTSTANDING PLAYER —
John Joiner, Leesville

COACH-OF-THE-YEAR —
Keith Andrews, Leesville

1974
Ken Hughes

1975
Randall Smith

1973
Floyd Tinsley

1974
1973 Johnny Walters
1973 Ricky Shaw

PAT LYNCH
6'3" Senior
Free Throw Percentage Leader

Leland Bennett

Bobby McIntosh

Pat Williams

Gary McDonald

Gary McDonald scores 46 points

ROBERT BLOW - 6'2" Guard, Sr. Made the 1st team 3-AA All-District. Was a leading rebounder and scorer. Won the Lions Club Award for Outstanding Play this season.

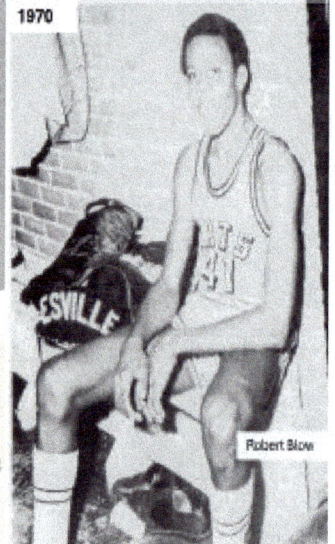

Robert Blow

1969 ALL-DISTRICT 3-AA TEAM

First Team
Player, School	Ht.	Class	Votes
Tynes Hildebrand, Natchitoches	5-11	Senior	30
Stan Beeson, Pineville	5-10	Senior	30
Skeeter Salim, Natchitoches	5-8	Senior	28
Terry Copeland, Jena	6-0	Senior	28
Gary Sellers, Tioga	5-10	Senior	26

Second Team
James Smith, Pineville
Asa Skinner, Leesville
Ronnie Price, Marksville
Steve Hall, Marksville
Robert Neblett, Menard

Third Team
Gary McDonald, Leesville
Billy Tucker, Jena
Steve Laurence, Leesville
Gordon Ducote, Menard
Danny Snow, Menard
Johnny Fain, Tioga

Outstanding Player — Tynes Hildebrand, Natchitoches.
Outstanding Coach — Bobby Rucker, Pineville

1960
Steve Laurence (44) & James Leech (24)

1968
Vic Ortiz, Asa Skinner, Steve Laurence, Coach Bobby Craft, Ralph Irving, James Leech
Starting Five

1968

3-AA All-District 1967

1967 DISTRICT 3-AA TEAM
FIRST TEAM
Player, School	Ht.	Wt.	Class
Allen Posey, Natchitoches	6-2	161	Senior
Ronnie Haworth, Natchitoches	6-3	190	Senior
Ronnie Melder, Menard	6-0	165	Senior
Russell Moore, Tioga	6-0	155	Senior
Tim Lynch, Leesville	6-2	170	Senior

SECOND TEAM
Player, School	Ht.	Wt.	Class
Doug Williams, Tioga	6-0	155	Senior
Jim Rudd, DeRidder	6-5	180	Senior
Perry Futrell, Pineville	5-10	170	Senior
Larry Witherell, Tioga	6-0	165	Senior
Charles Randell, Menard	6-0	145	Senior

OUTSTANDING PLAYER—Allen Posey, Natchitoches.
OUTSTANDING COACH—Derwood Duke, Natchitoches.
HONORABLE MENTION: Roy Lofton, Leesville; Luke Thomas, Natchitoches; Joey Crouch, Pineville; Rodney Lofton, Pineville; Gary Parker, DeRidder; Mac McKinley, DeRidder.

LEESVILLE (62)					
Player	GA-M	FA-M	RB	PF	TP
Lynch	10-7	8-7	13	2	21
Irving	21-5	5-3	3	3	13
Leech	6-2	0-0	3	5	4
Ortiz	7-3	1-0	3	4	6
Lofton	11-5	10-8	18	3	18
Nash	0-0	0-0	0	1	0
White	0-0	0-0	1	1	0
Totals	66-22	24-18	43	19	62
DeRIDDER (54)					
Bradley	6-5	8-4	4	1	14
McKinley	17-6	3-2	2	2	14
Hyde	3-1	6-5	1	2	7
Parker	5-4	2-1	12	5	9
Rudd	2-2	7-5	5	5	9
Scarborough	0-0	2-1	0	0	1
Pernici	0-0	0-0	1	1	0
Totals	33-18	28-18	25	16	54

Score by Quarters:
Leesville 8 25 36 51 62
DeRidder 17 21 34 51 54

1967

The 1969-70 Wampus Cat Basketball Team made history as they were the first Leesville team to make the state play-offs since the Cats became an AA school in 1959.

The Cats were 11-1 in district and 23-11 for the full season. After tying Pineville for the District Championship the Cat Cagers lost in a special play-off and had to travel for the first state play-off game. After leading for most of the game, the Cats lost to the eventual State Champs, the DeRidder Dragons.

The Wampus Cats won the Civitan Parish tournament and also won second in the L. H. S. Round Robin tournament.

This was a fine Wampus Cat basketball team and one that we will always be proud of.

1970

DISTRICT 3-AA ALL-DISTRICT

Player, School	Ht.	Cl.	Avg.
Ronnie Price, Pineville	6-2	Sr.	20.8
Vic Sooter, Pineville	5-10	Sr.	17.1
Gary MacDonald, Leesville	6-2	Sr.	23.0
Kim Luker, Natchitoches	6-2	Sr.	17.7
Robert Blow, Leesville	6-1	Sr.	14.2

SECOND TEAM

Player, School	Ht.	Cl.	Avg.
Vince O'Brien, Tioga	6-3	Jr.	19.9
Elmer Maxey, Tioga	6-6	Jr.	16.2
Steve Hall, Marksville	6-4	Sr.	19.5
Robert Neblett, Menard	6-0	Jr.	16.5
Danny Snow, Menard	6-2	Jr.	15.3

OUTSTANDING PLAYERS — Vic Sooter and Ronnie Price, Pineville.
COACH OF THE YEAR — Bobby Rucker, Pineville.
Third Team — Gene Knecht, Natchitoches; Alfred Gay, Natchitoches; Johnny Greene, Menard; Billy Sharbano, Jena; Quinton Aucoin, Jena; Steve Lawrence, Leesville.

1970

DISTRICT 3-AA STANDINGS

Team	W.	L.	Pct.
Leesville	9	0	1.000
Pineville	8	1	.888
Menard	4	3	.571
Natchitoches	4	5	.444
Tioga	3	5	.375
Jena	1	8	.111
Marksville	0	7	.000

Tuesday's Results
Leesville 69, Natchitoches 67
Pineville 70, Tioga 68
Menard 86, Jena 15

Friday's Schedule
Tioga at Leesville
Jena at Marksville
Natchitoches at Menard
Pineville at Rapides (Saturday)

Prep Scene

by 1970

Paul Wappler

Drum Major Leesville Cage Star

Steve Lawrence has this thing about whistles.

During the football season Lawrence blows a whistle and the Leesville Wampus Cat band strikes up and marches on the field. When roundball time comes around, the referee has the whistle and it gives Lawrence and the rest of the Cat cage team a time to relax.

Lawrence is the Wampus Cat drum major during the football season, although he doesn't fit the picture of a show leader.

Lawrence stands right at 6-4, and tips the scales at 175. He is muscular and looks like he would be a perfect running back. He hasn't played on the gridiron since he was a sophomore.

On the hardwood, Lawrence, a senior, has started for three years. This season he is hitting on a 19-point clip which ranks him second behind Gary MacDonald.

Wampus Cat head coach Ricky Reese stated the other day, "Steve is a real dedicated player. He and Gary MacDonald are two of the hardest workers I've ever seen."

Lawrence and the Cats will meet Pineville tonight in the District 3-AA cage feature of the year. A Leesville win and they should have a perfect record in the first half of the round-robin. A Pineville win and the Cats are backed up against the wall.

Nobody can remember the last time Leesville took top honors in 3-AA basketball.

This year, with a drum major pulling the strings, the Cats have a real good shot at it. Real good. Just ask Bobby Rucker how good.

1966

Joe Gendron (40) and John Henson (32)

Basketball Lettermen Chosen
1966

The players who received letters in basketball this year are as follows: John Henson, guard; James Latham, guard, center; David Smith, guard; Billy Sexson, guard; Joe Gendron, forward; Tim Lynch, forward; Roger Causey, forward; Prentiss Dixon, guard; Ralph Irving, guard; Wayne Riddle, manager; and Bruce Wheatley, trainer.

John Henson, senior and captain of the team, was the only three year letterman. James Latham and David Smith have lettered two years.

Those receiving a letter for the first time are as follows: Joe Gendron, varsity; Tim Lynch, varsity; Billy Sexson, varsity; Roger Causey, junior varsity; Prentiss Dixon, junior varsity; Ralph Irving, junior varsity; Wayne Riddle, and Bruce Wheatley

1965

ALL-STAR basketball players from Leesville High School in District 3-AA are Junior Temple (right), first team forward, and Tom Adams, second team center.

1965

Tom Adams (52)

1964

L.H.S. says good-bye to Coach Bennett and thanks him for a job well done.   232 Wins

All-District 3-AA
1964

Player, School	Class	Ht.	Wt.
Ronnie Kaiser, Pineville	Sr.	6-5	200
Richard Schwartz, Leesville	Sr.	5-10	150
Mike Taylor, Jena	Sr.	6-4	185
Glenn Randow, Pineville	Sr.	6-2	180
Jay Pierson, Natchitoches	Sr.	6-0	160

SECOND TEAM	THIRD TEAM
Buck Williams, Tioga	Sid Cannon, Jena
Steve Boniol, Menard	Junior Temple, Leesville
Hap Plauche, Pineville	Pat Dunham, Natchitoches
Tony Tarpley, Jena	Danny Dortherow, Tioga
Billy Crawford, Leesville	Robert Cyphert, Pineville

All-District 3-AA — 1963

Player, Team	Pos.	Class	Ht.	Votes
David Clark, Natchitoches	F	Senior	6-3	25
Mike Arrington, Tioga	F	Senior	6-2	25
Tim Hall, Menard	C	Senior	6-4	25
Edwin Cabra, Leesville	G	Senior	5-10	23
Don Bates, Pineville	G	Senior	5-9	20

SECOND TEAM
Leslie Windham, Jena
Glenn Randow, Pineville
Richard Schwartz, Leesville
Marvin Brosset, Menard
Mike Taylor, Jena
Ronnie Kaiser, Pineville

THIRD TEAM
Jay Pierson, Natchitoches
LeRoy Joiner, Jena
Calvin Long, Tioga
Frank Duke, Tioga
Harold LeBlanc, Menard

Natchitoches 74, Leesville 67

Natchitoches	16	42	53	74
Leesville	16	28	45	67

NATCHITOCHES (74) — Beyer 6, Clark 23, Nesom 9, Taylor 16, Pierson 7, Chester 13, Deason.

LEESVILLE (67) — Cabra 31, Schwartz 25, Magee, Temple 4, Crawford 7.

Senior Players — 1962
Danny Hardwick, Bobby Craft, Wade Norris, Winthrop Winborn, Paul Shaw.

Louis Magee — 1963

All-District 3-AA — 1962

Player, School	Class	Ht.	Votes
Kenny Arthur, Natchitoches	12	6-2	29
Ernie Knobloch, Menard	12	6-2	25
Danny Hardwick, Leesville	12	5-9	25
Mike Arrington, Tioga	11	6-1	21
Tim Hall, Menard	11	6-4	19

Second Team
Calvin Long, Tioga (17)
Bobby Craft, Leesville (17)
Joe Beasley, Natchitoches (16)
Ross Gwinn, Natchitoches (16)
David Bates, Pineville (14)
LeRoy Joiner, Jena (14)

Third Team
Wayne Martin, Pineville (12)
David Clark, Natchitoches (8)
Ray Attner, Pineville (3)
Leslie Windham, Jena (3)
Doug Fine, Pineville (3)
Ronnie Kaiser, Pineville (3)

ALL-STATE CLASS AA — 1961

Player, Team	Ht.	Class
Richard Reese, Leesville	6-2	12
Charles Sheffield, Ruston	6-1	11
Al Setton, Ponchatoula	5-7	12
Bob Cutrer, Baker	6-1	12
Jerry Hood, Ruston	6-4	12

Second Team
Barry Ackel, Menard
Wayne Collier, North Caddo
Bob Methvin, Natchitoches
Wayne Patterson, Covington
Ronnie Small, Denham Springs

Third Team
Ken Arthur, Natchitoches
Jerry Joe Dunaway, Glen Oaks
A. C. Vitter, Ponchatoula
Jerry Benit, Minden
Buddy Morgan, Springhill

Player-of-Year—Richard Reese, Leesville
Coach-of-Year—Tynes Hildebrand, Natchitoches

SENIORS — 1961
L-R Sid Morris, John Raford, Ronald Parker, Richard Reese, Gene Cavanaugh

STATISTICS — 1961

Games played	35
Games won	28
Games lost	7
Total points scored	2339
Total points against	1814
Offensive average	66.8
Defensive average	54.6

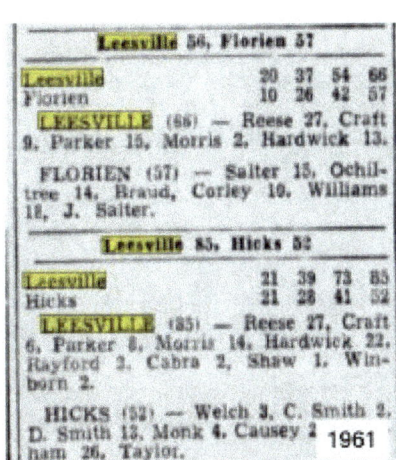

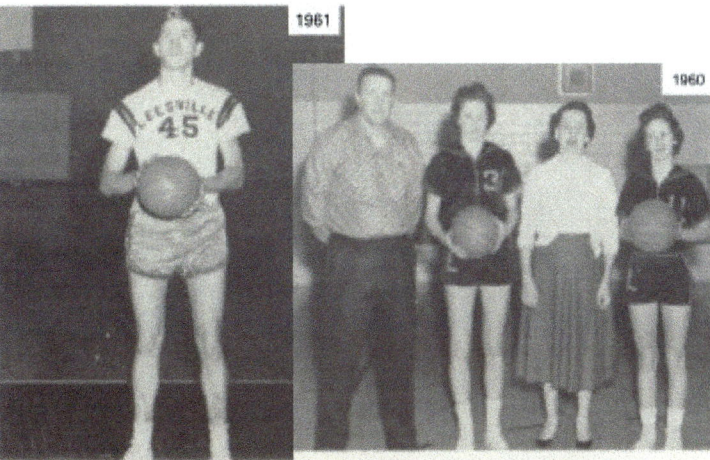

Carolyn Holifield, Coach Rhodes, Judy Cavanaugh

Seniors

BETSY MAY
Co-Captain - Forward

Cat Teams Lose In State Cage Playoffs

Leesville High School boys and girls teams were defeated last Friday night in the first round of the state basketball playoffs.

Tioga's girls dropped the Leesville girls by a score of 41 to 33, while the Tioga boys downed the Wampus Cat boys team 45 to 32.

Barbara Huffinton and Sharon Ford led Tioga with 19 and 13 points while Gail Bridges and Betsy May led Leesville's scoring attack with 18 and 11.

Rodney Robertson and John Delk led Tioga's boys in scoring with 13 and 10 points, while J. C. Welch collected 10 points and 13 rebounds for the Wampus Cats.

LEWIS MASSEY

Pollock Girls Bow; Leesville Trips Oakdale
1957

Pollock's girls bowed to Mangham, defending state Class B basketball champion, Tuesday night, 72-47, in a sectional playoff game.

Meanwhile, the Class A bi-districts were launched with Leesville, champion of 4-A, spilling 3-A runnerup Oakdale 32-18.

Leesville will play the Lake Providence - Winnfield winner in the regionals by next Tuesday.

Mangham, with its starting line-up from last year intact, pulled away from Pollock in the second half Tuesday. Pollock trailed by only six points at one stage of the third period.

Catherine Arrant piled up 44 points for Mangham to lead all scorers. Earlene McKay was high for Pollock with 34.

Mangham meets Martin Friday night in the Class B semi-finals. Martin defeated Baskin 63-58 Tuesday.

Jeanne Beltz led Leesville past Oakdale with 15 points. Louise Ritchie scored nine for the losers.

JEANIE BELTZ
Forward

Leesville Is 44-38 Victor
1956

MERRYVILLE La., (Spl.) — Merryville's Panthers dropped a close 44-38 decision to the Leesville Wampus Cats in the final basketball game of the season for the Merryville quintet here Thursday night.

Leesville will close out its campaign Tuesday night with a game at Hornbeck.

LEESVILLE	G	F	P	MERRYVILLE	G	F	P
Hrdwick	0	10-10	2	Ramsey	5	6-16	5
Nalley	5	3-4	3	Calhoun	2	0-0	3
West	6-0	1	Jacobs	1	0-0	1
Bolgiano	4	0-1	1	Jeans	2	0-2	1
Welch	1	0-1	4	Meadows	5	0-4	3
Arthur	1	1-2	1				
Allen	1	2-4	2				
Totals	14	16-20	14	Totals	15	8-22	11

SCORE BY QUARTERS
Leesville .... 8 14 14 14—44
Merryville .... 2 8 16 12—38

SHIRLEY CAVANAUGH - Captain
GELENA SCOGGINS - Captain

RECORD FOR SEASON
Games won - 28
Games lost - 11
39

DON GOINS - Guard

JIMMY EDWARDS - Forward

Leesville placed first in the Leesville tournament and second in the Pitkin tournament. There were only two lettermen on this year's team, Jimmy Edwards and Don Goins.

Co-Captains
DON GOINS - JIMMY EDWARDS

LHS Lady Cats 1954

RECORD FOR SEASON
Games won - 29
Games lost - 1
Total points scored:
Leesville - 1468
Opponents - 711

CLASS A GIRLS (Semi-Finals)

LEESVILLE (66)	fg	ft	pf	MT. CARMEL	fg	ft	pf
Truax	21	4	5	Campbell	7	5	
Cavanaugh	5	2	1	Owens	9	5	
Jones	1	2	1	Calais	7	8	
Jacobs	0	0	0	Safford	0	0	
Scoggins	1	2	0	B. Landry	6	1	
Jeane	0	0	4	Durand	0	0	
Whittaker	0	0	4	M. Landry	0	0	
Mont'ery	0	0	2				
Hardwick	0	0	5				
Boigiano	0	0	5				
	28	10	27		7	19	

Score by periods:
Leesville .... 15 16 20 15—
Mt. Carmel .... 5 9 5 14—

Class A Girls All-State Basketball Team — 1954

F—Glenda Bennett, Winnsboro
F—Shirley Williams, Winnsboro
F—Voncell Bracknell, Tioga
F—Shirley Cavanaugh, Leesville
F—M. A. Trahant, Amite
F—Kainia Manitzas, DeRidder
G—Bessie Wairon, Winnsboro
G—Winona Starnes, Tioga
G—Geneva Williams, Winnsboro
G—Faye Jeane, Leesville
G—Shirley Graves, Tioga

1954

1953

LARRY GOINS

Jane Carey
All State '51

Class A' All-State Selections 1953
Boys
Travis Ford, Jonesboro, forward.
Harmon Ayres, Jonesboro, forward.
Star Stumpf, Newman, center.
Leon Greenblatt, Newman, guard.
Ralph Richardson, Springhill, guard.
Ever Sandlin, Leesville, center.
John Crowe, Springhill, center.
Earl McClain, Covington, guard.
Phinn Kennon, Jena, center.
Bobby Booth, Hammond, center.

Girls
First team.
Forwards — Glenda Bennett, Winnsboro, Ann Crawford, Winnsboro, Gretchen Kovac, Oak Grove.
Guards—Gwendolyn Whittaker, Leesville; Mitzie Roberts, Winnfield; Yvonne Cromwell, LaSalle.
Second team:
Forwards — Mary Trahant, Amite; Shirley Hayers, Many; Audrey Chamberlain, Leesville.
Guards — Beth Landry, Mt. Carmel of Lafayette; Dorothy Williams, Winnsboro; Faye Jeane, Leesville.

All-State Team 1952
GIRLS
1. F—Margie Caskey, Homer.
2. F—Geraldine Bradway, Oak
3. F—Betty Paddy, Leesville.
4. F—Mary Alice Trahant, Amite.
5. F—Shirley Domingue, Scott.
6. F—Edwina Vining, Amite.
7. G—Ravena Flynn, St. Joseph's, Baton Rouge.
8. G—Johnny Louise Frazier, Winnfield.
9. G—Fay Jeane, Leesville.
10. G—Verna Simmons, Amite.
11. G—Pat Stiles, Gretna.
12. G—Emma Jean Mosley, Oak Grove.

All-State Team 1951
Girls
Peggy Crain, Pine; Willies Walthall, Oak Grove; Betty Paddy, Leesville; Ida Lee Pierce, Oak Grove; Imogene Mosely, Oak Grove; June Carey, Leesville; Arlene Leger, Scott; Etta Pearl Dommiaque, Scott; Nettie Lou Simmons, Pine; Ann Crawford, Winnsboro; Mary Clarie Case, Amite; Patsey Brooks, Bastrop; Sue Grappe, Many.

All-State Performers

Boys

1931	Johnny Pelt
1953	Elber Sandell
1958 & 1959	Dale Hardwick
1961	Richard Reese
1964	Richard Schwartz
1983	Nikita Wilson
1987	Michael Joiner
1991	Patrick Kennedy
1995 & 96	Demond Mallet
1996	Reggie Degray
1998	JJ Joiner
1999	Derek Wright
2000	Darnell Bradley
2001 & 2002	Eric Woods
2019	Duwon Tolbert

Michael Joiner

JJ Joiner

Demond Mallet

Duwon Tolbert

Nikita Wilson

Richard Reese

Eric Woods

Dale Hardwick

Shonte Kennedy

Gwyn Whittaker

All-State Performers

Girls

1951	Betty Paddy
1951	Jane Carry
1953 & 1954	Faye Jean
1953	Gwendolyn Whittaker
1953	Audrey Chamberlain
1954	Shirley Cavanaugh
1998	Angela Davidson
2001	Sheronda Bowers
2003 & 2004	Shonte Kennedy
2010	Tiffany Wallace
2011	Chelsea Martin
2018	Kerrigan Small

Shirley Cavanaugh

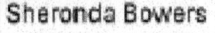
Sheronda Bowers

Angela Davidson

Faye Jeane

Tiffany Wallace

The Rich History of Leesville High School

Hopefully, this book on the history of Wampus Cat basketball will inspire others to craft histories of other aspects of the Old School on the Hill. The school in Vernon Parish has been both an incubation center and a launching pad for many great citizens in our State and country. LHS has also been the home of many great organizations, events and served as a focal point for the entire community.

Graduates of Leesville High School have achieved positions of esteem and acclaim in State and Federal Government. Suzette Kuhlow Kent (1986 graduate) served as the Chief Information officer of the United States in the late 2010s; two other Wampus Cats, 1986 graduate Jon Howerton and 1984 graduate Ronald Clark remain on active duty as general officers in the United States Army. Cindy Haygood, class of 85, is a general officer in the Louisiana National Guard. 1978 Graduate David Smith, a career Army officer (and Wampus Cat football player) twice appeared on the cover of LIFE Magazine, most prominently in the middle of DESERT STORM. 1951 graduate Guy Stone was the recipient of the Navy Cross for gallantry in the Vietnam War. 1980 graduate Sam Cox. Wampus Cat basketball player recently retired as a Lieutenant General from the United States Air Force.

LTC (R) David Smith

LtGen (R) Sam Cox

LTG Ronald Clark

BG Cindy Haygood

BG Jon Howerton

Guy Stone, SEAL
Navy Cross

Two LHS grads have served as US Congressmen (Jim McCrery, Class of 67 & Claude Leach (1951 graduate). Carolyn Leach Huntoon served as the Director of NASA's Johnson Space Center in Houston, making her the first female to head a Space Center in the US government. Garland Riddle, Class of 67 is an Emmy-nominated costume designer who had a 30+ year in the television and movie business. Larrie King, Class of 2001, is a professor of Art & Design at Kent State. 1972 graduate Tony McDonald led a US contingent to the Havana Arts Biennial in Cuba in 2015.

Cong Jim McCrery   Cong Buddy Leach   Caroly Leach Huntoon   Tony McDonald

Ted Castillo went on to a Hall of Fame career as a sportswriter in Baton Rouge and still attended LHS Homecomings until his passing in 2023. Academically, LHS remains consistently ranked high in the State of Louisiana. LHS has produced graduates of all US service academies and has sent students to colleges throughout the world. Countless National Merit Scholarship have come forth from years in the black and gold and millions of dollars of scholarships for college and technical training have been awarded to LHS students.

Wampus Cat athletes have achieved great things in other sports, including football, baseball, softball. track and field, soccer, swimming, cross country and other sports. Without question, the presence of the Wampus Cat Marching Band, cheerleaders, majorettes, dance line, JROTC and other auxiliary organizations make Leesville High School a special place.

So much history could be written on all of these topics and this author hopes others will endeavor to document what has taken place. Not mentioning or deep-diving in to these topics is not meant to disparage nor take away from the other wonderful things that have taken place at Leesville High School.

Leesville High School Sports Hall of Fame

In 2012, the Leesville High School Alumni Association created a Leesville High School Sports Hall of Fame. Since that time, the Association has inducted 13 former Wampus Cats into the Hall. The parameters for nomination and induction are listed at the Association's website, www.wampuscats.org. Nominations are open year-round and the induction takes places each year at the LHS Homecoming in the Fall. Athletes and coaches from football, basketball, track, and baseball have been inducted. The athlete/coach and year of induction are below.

Kevin Mawae, 2012
Football

Eddie Fuller 2013
Football

Richard Reese, 2014
Basketball & Coaching

Family of Ted Paris, 2014
Football & Coaching,
Posthumously

Leesville High School Sports Hall of Fame - Continued

Robert Gaines, 2015
Track & Football

Terry Holt, 2016
Football & Track

Grant Westerchil, 2017
Basketball & Coaching

Holly Wentz-Reeves, 2018
Track & Cross Country

TB Porter, 2019
Football

Demond Mallet, 2020
Basketball & Baseball

Leesville High School Sports Hall of Fame - Continued

Greg Fontenot, 2021
Baseball

Nikita Wilson, 2022
Basketball

Donald Mallet & Cordelia Thomas, accepting for
Coach Foster Thomas, 2022
Posthumous Induction

Leesville High School Sports Hall of Fame - Continued

Keith Zinger, 2023
Football

Faye Jean West, 2024
Girls' Basketball – Posthumously

Cecil Collins, 2024
Football

Special Section: Quick Highlights of Other Great Teams, Athletes and Coaches at Leesville School

This book is about basketball, but it is the author's hope that this effort will inspire others to join in and fully document the other accomplishments in other sports by fellow Wampus Cats. Given the fact that many other great, interesting and often inspiring things have taken place at Leesville High School, it seems fitting to pay some tribute to some of the other sports at the school. This section provides some highlights of some of the most prolific teams and athletes in Wampus Cat history. While many great and breath-taking things have taken place at LHS, to keep this manageable we'll have to mostly limit what we write here to other state championship teams, state runner ups, semi-finalists and stellar individual accomplishments, such as achieving All-State and All-American honors. Nothing is intentionally omitted. It should also be noted that compiling such information is time-consuming and we REALLY hope others will step forward in helping getting all of LHS Sports documented to a reasonable degree, like we've done for football and basketball.

Football

All this information is documented in LHS Wampus Cat Football History, but we'll provide a quick review he3re. There are two teams that stand out as the greatest in Wampus Cat Football History, 1995 and 2018. In 1995, the Cats went 13-2 on the season, won their district outright and made it all the way to the State Finals in the Super Dome. Danny Smith coached this squad and the team sported 3 on the All State roster: Cecil Collins, Greg Rone and Dennis Fetting. Cecil Collins was named LHSAA's Mr. Football. All District performers were: Fetting (OL), Collins (RB), Rone (LB), Shermaine Jones (DB), Robert Carter (DL), Sig Milerski (DL), Ced Clemons (LB) and Mike Lewis (DB).

In 2018, the Cats went 13-1 on the year and made it all the way to the State Semi-Finals. The Wampus Cats won 13 games in a row and lost only in the Semi-Finals to eventual champion Warren Easton. Robert Causey, who, as this writing, is the most accomplished coach in Wampus Cat football history was head man on the sidelines. Matthew Anderson (OL) was named First Team All State and Coach Causey was State Coach of the Year. All District performers were Caleb Gallashaw (RB), D'ante Gallashaw (RB & Offensive MVP), Montae Lynch (OL), Anderson (OL), Brett Pope (C), Darius Sawyer (ATH & KR), Jacob Mount (QB), Noah Allain (TE), Khrystian Hoffpauir (WR), Peyton Lipps (OL) Ben Ward (P), Talyn Adams (DL), Nick Green (DL), Matt Pajinag (LB), Darius Allen (LB), Aaron Hunter (DL), Ruben Jeane (DL), Jacob Feliciano (DB), Nigel McCoy (DB), and Efosa Evbuomwan (FLEX).

Leesville's most decorate player in the sport of football is Kevin Mawae. The 1989 LHS graduate was All-State for Leesville, lettered 4 years at LSU, had a long and successful career in the NFL and was later inducted into the LHS Sports Hall of Fame, the LHSAA Sports Hall of Fame, the Louisiana Sports Hall of Fame and the Professional Football Hall of Fame.

Cecil Collins & Denni Fetting　　　Robert Causey　　　Kevin Mawae

Rodeo

Though mentioned earlier in the book, the accomplishment LHS athletes in the sport of rodeo merits additional review. The Porter sisters (Judy, Cathy and Lindy) and Judy Stokes (Class of 1968) achieved state-wide and national acclaim and notoriety in rodeo during the period of time when no sports were offered at LHS for girls. The athleticism required to do rodeo-type of events is significant. Riding and maneuvering a horse at full speed and then conducting hand-eye skills such as roping a calf or turning a full-speed animal on a dime in barrel racing is both highly complex and dangerous. The Porter girls and their younger brother David and Miss Stokes were acclaimed in Louisiana and in pockets around the country as some of the best in the sport at the time. Judy was the top cowgirl in the State for four years. Cathy and Lindy were also state champions and Lindy was in the top 3 in the nation in the event of break-away roping in her senior year at LHS. From 1966 – 1974, one of the Porter girls was the All-Around Cowgirl in Louisiana in every year except one. Stokes was a two-time state champion in 1967 and 68.

  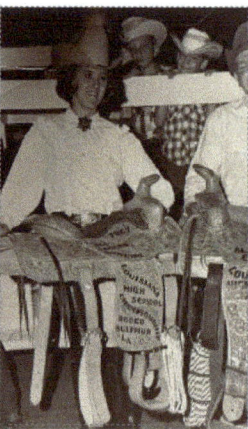 

Judy Stokes　　　Cathy Porter　　　Judy Porter

Track and Field

Leesville has had many great track and field athletes and a number of superb teams. Boys' Track and Field won 2 x State Championships, and was State Runner-Up once. The 1978 team was coach by Rolf Kuhlow and 1980s squad was led by Coach Randy Price. The 78 squad was the first team in the history of LHS to win a state title. On the 78 squad, 4 athletes were named All-American: Cedric Johnson, Terry Sparks, Terry Holt and Robert Gaines. Those 4, plus Carl Clark (440 relay), Jerry Lynch (jumps), Michael Johnson (long jump) and Jimbo Pawlik (distance) were named All-State in that season.

1978 Boys' State Track Champions

In 1980, Robert Gaines was linchpin to one of the most dramatic moments in LHS history and that moment merits noting. Heading into the final event of the evening, the Cats needed to win the 4 x 400 relay to win the state championship. Gaines, a six-time State champion and 12 time All-State selection (top 3 in an event) took the baton as the anchor leg and was down by nearly 40 yards at the beginning of the last lap. Robert ran a 46.9 final leg in the relay to help the Cats secure their 2nd title in 3 years. Also an acclaimed football player and basketball letterman, Gaines went on to a record setting career as a sprinter at McNeese. Other All-State performers from that team included Levon White, Bernard Matthews, Victor Roberson. Oscar Joiner and Leon Jackson.

1980 Boys' Track Team: State Champions

The 1999 Wampus Cat boys' track team finished second at the State Meet to Opelousas. The 99 squad was led by 2 x State Champion relay teams---the 800 and 1600 M relay teams and individual stat champion Keith Smith in the 400M. Smith, also an All- State football player would go on to a highly successful college football career and then 8 years in the NFL. All-State performers on the meet included Smith, Macklin Mcray (4x400), Deshun McNeely (4x200 and 4x 400), Jonathan Hopkins (4x200 and Triple Jump, and Jay Preston (4x 400). Others notching points on this day included Justin Brown in the Triple Jump and Derek Beebee in the 200M.

| 1980 | 1999 | 2006 |

In 2006, the Wampus Cats finished second at the LHSAA State Meet. Discus thrower Scott Ewes and high jumper Anthony Craft brought home individual titles. Sprinter and football star Bernardo Henry brought home points in the 200 meter dash (21.59) and joined Casetti Brown, Craft and Cornellli Jackson in a runner-up spot on the 4 x 100 relay. The Cats also got points from Justin Ford in the high jump and Ewes notched additional points in the shotput. "Chop" Thomas was the coach during this season.

Scott Ewes | Bernardo Henry

On the girls' side, the Lady Cats achieved State Runner-Up status in 1982. The 82 team was coached by Troy Howard. Of note on the 82 squad was Holly Wentz (now Reeves). Holly is the first LHS female athlete to be named All-American. She broke the state record in the 800 meter run in her sophomore year and the record stood for over a decade. Holly went on to a successful career at Wheaton College and earned NAIA All-American honors and was later enshrined as the first Lady Wampus Cat in the LHS Sports Hall of Fame (in 2018). Pat James, Francis Sparks and Mechelle Bowman were All-State performers on this squad, as well.

Back Row, Left to Right: Holly Wentz, Tina Miller, Denise Burnett, Meshalle Schapell, Connie Howard, Palice Gray, Regina Dixon, Jenise Cormier, Beth Genega, Francis Sparks, Coach Howard, Front Row, Left to Right: Mashian Brown, Cynthia Howard, Kathy Stuart, Shelia Ford

1982 Girls' Track Team: State Runner-Up

Cross Country

In 2013, the LHS Boys' Cross Country Team finished 2nd in the LHSAA State Meet. Coach Joe Severino's squad finished second to Assumption in the meet, edging out defending champion Benton who finished 3rd. Nicholas Teague finished third overall and Andrew Barefield finished 9th, earning both athletes' All-State honors. Other members of the team included Brett Schmidt, Jeresun Atkin, Connor Morgan Call, Isaac Ayala and Jesse St. Clergy.

Softball

The Lady Cats Softball team of 2012 came within an eyelash of winning the State Championship. Coach Kelly Kaiama-Goodwin's team advanced to the state championship by defeating Plaquemine, Deridder, Neville, Academy of Our Lady, then losing a close game to Teurlings Catholic 7-6 in the title game. The squad started slowly on the year but came on strong finishing the season with a record of 18-13, but the team made its mark on state softball. McKenna Goodwin was named All-State on the season. Ashley Hoecker, Haley Magee, Karsen Kreps and Chelsei Alexander were All-District performers on the season. Coach Kiama-Goodwin was named Coach of the Year for the effort.

Pictured below: Bottom: Principal Renita Page, Hannah Doyal, Tajai McCollum, Chelsei Alexander, Haley Magee, Ali Williams, Manager Haley McConathy, Top: Coach Kelly Kaiama-Goodwin, Ashley Hoecker, McKenna Goodwin, Karsen Kreps, Camille Hamilton, Elaine Blanco, Coach Joe Sowells

2012 Girls' Softball Team: State Runner-Up

Baseball

The most successful baseball team in LHS history that can be documented was the 1997 squad that advanced the State Semi-Finals. Coach Bruce Stewart's squad, who had finished the season 3rd place in the district advanced through the playoffs and lost a heartbreaker to John Curtis 8-4 at home in the semis. The 1997 team defeated West Ouachita and ASH on the way to the Final 4 in the state. Junior Derek Mayo, probably the winningest pitcher in LHS history was joined by JJ Joiner, Tim Johnson, Keith Lawton, and Marcus Thurman on the All-District team. Mayo was a two-time, First Team All-State pitcher for the Wampus Cats.

Cat teams that advanced to the quarterfinals were in 1974, 1982 and 1996. The 74 team was coached by Ricky French, the 82 squad was coached by Tom Neubert and the 96 team was led by Bruce Stewart. Stars from the 74 squad included Mike Paris, Jerry Bynog, Ray Macias and Ricky Shaw. From the 82 included future LHS Hall of Famer and LSU star Greg Fontenot, John Lafosse, Wayne Hicks, WL Bynog and Reggie Bennett. The 96 squad featured Demond Mallet, Crispin Craft, Jason Green, and JJ Joiner. The 1998 team went 23-6 on the year and probably achieved the highest win total in LHS history. Mayo went 11- 0 on that season and signed to play collegiately after graduation.

Also of note in Leesville baseball were players who went on to significant success in college and earned chances to play in the major leagues. Dustin Smith, who lettered 4 years at McNeese played in the Chicago Cubs organization; Justin

Cryer who played at Ole Miss earned a spot in the Blue Jays organization; and Johnathon Harmon, who played at Northwestern and in the Cincinnati Reds' organization.

Derek Mayo, Two-Time All-State   Justin Cryer   Dustin Smith

1997 Wampus Cat Baseball Team

Back Row, Left to Right: Mark Holtsberry, Jim Capbell, John Lafosh, Jimbo Shapkoff, Luther Mouth, Cowboy Scott, Ron Williams, Greg Fontenot. Front Row, Left to Right: Terry Ward, Reggie Bennett, Wyne Hicks, Paul McGee, Paul Kulama, W. L. Boynog, Ron Clark, T. J. Moore, Dirk Anderson.

1982 Wampus Cat Baseball Team

1974 Wampus Cat Baseball Team

Tennis

We found no record of state or regional championship teams at LHS. The Cats did, however, have mixed doubles team who won the state championship in 1985. Ronnie Langford and Tiamaree Root brought home a title for the Wampus Cats.

Bolton Nette In AAA Stat

SHREVEPORT — Donnie Langford and Timaree Root of Leesville took a 6-4, 2-6, 6-1 win over Bolton's Derrick Toomey and Catherine Dawson to win the state Class AAA mixed doubles high school championships here Wednesday.

Hall of Famers

Several LHS graduates stand alongside football star Kevin Mawae as Hall of Famers in organizations around the state and the country. Each merit a brief and special mention

Vic Ortiz, LHS Class of 1969, is a member of the Louisiana High School Athletic Association (LHSAA) Hall of Fame as a coach. Vic (and most of his brothers) were football stars at LHS. Vic was also a basketball player and a key contributors on the field during his days as a Wampus Cat. After graduation from college, Coach Ortiz returned to Leesville where he coached football, freshman basketball and baseball for several seasons. In 1979, however, Vic left LHS for other coaching opportunities around the parish and he excelled in a tremendous way.

During a stint at Anacoco, Ortiz won 4 state championships in girls' basketball and one in track and field. During his time at Hicks High School, he won a girls' basketball championship and one in track and field. Upon retirement from the public school system, he took on coaching duties at Faith Training Academy, where he led the Lady Patriots basketball team to 3 State championships. In 2013, Coach Ortiz was inducted into the LHSAA Hall of Fame.

Ted Castillo, LHS Class of 1941, is a member of the Louisiana Sports Hall of Fame (headquartered in Natchitoches). After graduating as Valedictorian of LHS in 1941, Castillo went to LSU, where he was enrolled until he was drafted in 1942. He served in the US Navy and was decorated for his time in combat. After leaving college, Castillo finished a degree at LSU and began a 50+ year career as a journalist. He was the Advocate's lead High School Sports Reporter for over 50 years and contributed to the paper for over 70 years. He had the honor of interviewing LSU and Louisiana greats such as YA Title, Billy Cannon, Pete Maravich and Shaquille O'Neal, in addition to a litany of high school and college coaching greats. He covered Ron Guidry's World Series for the Advocate and also traveled to multiple national championship events and Super Bowls for the paper.

In 1985, he was inducted into the Louisiana Sports Hall of Fame in 1987 as a journalist. Castillo was an enthusiastic Wampus Cat who attended LHS Homecomings well into his 90s. He passed away in 2023.

T. Barrett Porter, LHS Class of 1946 is a member of multiple Halls of Fame around the country. A World Champion calf roper in 1949, Porter (known as "T-Berry") was inducted into the Rodeo Hall of Fame at the National Cowboy and Western Heritage Museum in Oklahoma City in 2015. In 2019 he was inducted into the LHS Sports Hall of Fame as a football player and in the Louisiana Sports Hall of Fame as the first Cowboy placed in the prestigious hall. Porter has been a linchpin citizen in Vernon Parish his entire life, running several businesses, raising cattle, being heavily involved in youth education related to agriculture and farming and for many years of service in the Leesville Lions Club.

Vic Ortiz   Ted Castillo   T.B. Porter

Demond Mallet, LHS Class of 1996 was inducted into the McNeese State University Hall of Fame in 2012. As mentioned previously in these pages, Demond was a genuine basketball star at LHS but he was a highly accomplished baseball player for the black and gold. At McNeese, he was an All-conference performer, was listed on the Cowboys' All-Decade team for the 1990s, and is one of the school's all-time leaders in scoring and assists. After college, Demond played professionally in Europe for over a decade. He was inducted into the LHS Sports Hall of Fame in 2020.

Holly Wentz-Reeves, LHS Class of 1984 is a member of the Hall of Honor at Wheaton College. As mentioned earlier in this chapter, Holly was a state champion and state record holder during her track days at Leesville. After high school, she attended and competed for Wheaton College in Illinois. Holly was a two-time qualifier for the NCAA Championships in the 800-meter run and was an All-American in the 800-meter run and on her school's 1600-meter relay team. She was inducted into the LHS Sports Hall of Fame in 2018.

ABOUT THE AUTHORS

This book has two primary authors, Billy Crawford and Charles Owen. Both are PROUD Wampus Cats and avid amateur historians.

Billy was graduated from LHS in 1964. He was a star basketball player, earning All-District honors in his senior season, playing for legendary coach Billy Bennett. Billy played alongside Richard Schwartz in Schwartz's record-breaking season when he poured in 29.3 points per game. Assists weren't tracked in those days, but it stands to reason that SOME of Richard's success came from Billy playing alongside him.

After graduation from college, Billy returned to LHS where he had an impactful career as a teacher, coach, then principal. He coached boys' basketball for a brief period and was the coach that former LHS Principal H.L Russell hand-picked to bring back girls' basketball at Leesville. Billy's service as Principal lasted six years, and he led LHS through some tumultuous days, ensuring academic excellence, discipline and pride were foundations at the Ole School on the Hill. After service in Vernon Parish, Billy served the people of Louisiana as a senior leader at the State Department of Education.

Charles Owen was graduated from LHS in 1981. He didn't play basketball after 9th grade, but was a great fan of the sport. He watched Keith Andrews' and Mike Mallet's team bring excitement to the LHS gym and fell in love with the sport. He did play football and ran track, but wasn't particularly noteworthy. Billy Crawford taught Charles Owen a fascinating course in American Government and helped light a fire of interest in the workings of government. After college at Louisiana Tech, Charles served in the United States Air Force for 20 years as a commissioned office and eventually found his way back to Leesville. He's married to 1985 LHS graduate Carolyn Van Dine, whose brother, Dennis played on the 75 Wampus Cat basketball team that won district with for Coach Andrews.

Billy and Charles both write stories about and track the history of Leesville High School.

Billy Crawford   Charles Owen

SOURCES & METHODS

This work was created and is carefully and intentionally identified as an "unofficial" history book. The book is not intended to be used as an academic source, nor is it endorsed, validated by any athletic or school governing body. This book was created as a gift to our hometown and is simply an attempt to document what could be found in terms of the history of Leesville High School basketball. A variety of sources and personal collections and recollections were used to compile this work. Below is a list of sources used in the creation of this book

1. Leesville Daily Leader, Hard Copy Files & Photos, stored at the Vernon Parish Library
2. Leesville Daily Leader, www.leesvilledailyleader.com
3. Newspapers.com, Newspapers + Publishers Extra: Retrieved from http://newspapers.com, various dates and various publications, including the Alexandria Daily Towntalk, Lake Charles American Press, Shreveport Times, Shreveport Journal, others
4. Vernon Parish Library, The Digital Archives Online: Retrieved from https:vernonarish.advantage-preservation.com
5. Leesville High School Yearbooks, various years
6. Smith, Rickie, Photographer
7. Wise, Eddie, Photographer
8. Personal Collections and contributions: Beth Westerchil, Jamal Brown, Edwin Cabra, Robert Carter

Index

A
Adams 130
Addison, 102
African American Head Coach, first, 14
Agatha Rhodes, 9, 11
Alexandria, 39, 47
Alexandria Daily Towntalk, 210
Alexandria Senior High, 19
Allain, Noah, 193
Allen, Norman 139
All-Around Cowgirl, 195
All-District and Coach Sowells, 29
Allen, Darius, 193
Allen, Norman, 40
All-State footballer Levander Liggins, 40
All-State honors, 18, 20, 24–25, 44, 47, 49, 201
All-State performers, 4, 13, 58, 197–99
All-State selection, 11, 38
All-State team, 27, 32, 42
all-time winningest coach in Leesville High School, 43
Alyse, 68
Alyse Lacking, 43
Amanda, 67
American Government, 209
Amite, 19, 62
Ammons, 65
Anacoco, 4–5, 40, 206
Anderson, 71, 193
  Matthew, 193
  Peter, 3
Andrews, 13–14, 50
  Jordan, 58
  Keith, 55, 63, 102, 103
Angela Davidson, 69
Angela Self, 22, 69–70
Angelina Jr, 48, 67
Angelina Junior College, 15, 18
Appelby, 113, 114
Apprentice School Builders, 49
ASH, 202
Assistant Coach Tracy Reese, 73
Assumption JaRielle James, 67

Averhart, 105
Ayala, Isaac, 201

B
Badger, 69
  Carissa, 28
Bailey, 125
Baker, 27, 60
Barefield, Andrew, 201
Ball, Darnell, 33
BASKETBALL CANCELLED, 71
Basketball for girls, 2
basketball star, former LHS, 16
Bastedo, 105, 106
Bastrop, 32, 38, 68
Baton Rouge, 24, 32, 34, 42, 45, 48, 73, 187
Beavers
  Bill 6
  Kim 104, 105
Beck, 113
beat Hammond, 59
beat Tara, 58
Beebee, Derek, 198
Beeson, 2, 66
Belaire, 48, 67
Beltz, 9, 86
Bennett, 8, 9, 53, 102, 105
  Bill, 53, 71
  Billy, 8–9, 22, 38, 54, 64–65, 71
  Reggie, 202
Berenson, 1
Berwick, 13, 101
Bishop Sullivan, 45
Blake, 39, 59, 132
  Jennifer, 42–43, 68
  Terrance, 38–39, 132
Blanco, Elaine, 201
Blow, Robert, 12–13, 64
Blue Jays organization, 204
Boerner, 21-22, 70, 109, 110
Bolgiano, 84. 86
Bolton, 40, 68
Bonin, 23, 29, 43, 53, 57, 69, 119
Boozer, 14, 102
Borrero, Yvette, 23, 114

Bossier, 32, 40, 44, 59
Bouya, R. 105, 106
Bowers, 32, 41, 127
Bowman, 109
Bradley, 32
   Darnell, 27, 32, 60, 125, 127
Bralie Fields, 48, 67
Brandon, 67
Brazil, 24, 102, 103
Breaux Bridge, 46, 58, 67
Broadmoor, 42, 68
Brock, Derrick, 45, 58
Brogen, Thelma, 3
Broocks, 29, 69
   Sherry, 29
Brown, Jamal, 210
Brown, James 125
Brown, Jeff, 27, 60
Brown, Deano 14, 102
Brown, Erwin, 21, 117
Broyles, 13
   Bill 13, 101
   Cindy 105
Brushes, 12
Bryant, 46, 58
Buchanan, 125
Bunch, Aubrey, 3
Burgess, 105
Burnett,114
Burley, Samuel, 73
Busheyhead, Lynn 104
Bustard, 130
Burns, 20, 62
Bursch
   Sam 14
   Sabrina 107
   Zeno 106
Burton, 21, 117
Bush, Edith, 3
Bush, Norris, 3
Buter, 128
Buter, Michael 108, 109
Bye, 72
Bynog,
   Darrell, 102
   Jerry, 202
   LD 84
Byrd, 29, 69

C
Cabra, Edwin, 10, 64, 210
Cage, D 105
Cain, 2
Caitlyn, 67
Caitlyn Sciarbarassi, 57
California, 1
Camile Canon, 46, 58
Campbell, Chris, 32, 34, 35, 36, 60, 73
Cannon, Billy, 206
Capitol, 24, 62
Captain Shreve, 20, 62
Carencro, 45, 58
Carey, Jane, 8, 72, 85
Carolos Pagan, 49
Carolyn Leach Huntoon, 187
Carolyn Van Dine, 209
Carr, Edna, 67
Carroll, 25, 61
Carte, Courtney, 42
Carter, 42, 47, 67–68. 132
   Courtney, 42, 68
   James, 36, 73
   Robert, 43, 47, 53, 193, 210
Carver, 34, 73
   defeated, 60
Cassetti Brown, 198
Castillo, 206
Cathedral, 66
Cathy, 11, 195
Cats and Lady Wampus Cats, 24
Cecilia, 45
Causey, Robert, 195
Cavanaugh, 71, 93, 130
   Shirley, 8
Cecilia, 58
Ced Clemons, 193
Centenary, 20, 62
Chamberlain, Audrey, 8, 71
Chelsea Martin All-State, 67
Chelsei Alexander, 201
Chicago Cubs organization, 202
Cincinnati Reds, 204

Clark, Carl, 197
Clark, Chad, 25
Clay, Kena, 31
Clayton, Rayford, 14
Cleary, Melissa, 23, 69
Clemons, 48, 57, 67
Clifton, 29, 69
   Tiffany, 28–29, 69
Coach Andrews, 13, 14, 63, 209
Coach Andrews Coach, 63
Coach Austin Temple, 3
Coach Billy Bennett, 9
Coach Bobby Craft, 10
Coach Bonin, 27–29, 69
Coach Brazil, 14
Coach Bruce Stewart, 202
Coach Caitlyn Gentry, 50
Coach Gentry, 50, 67
Coach Jimmy Leach, 10
Coach Joe Severino, 199
Coach Joe Sowells, 30, 40, 201
Coach Jordan, 19–20
Coach Josh Timberlake, 49
Coach Kay Taylor, 22
Coach Kelly Kaiama-Goodwin, 201
Coach Kiama-Goodwin, 201
Coach Mallet, 17–19, 22
Coach Mastro, 44–45
Coach Nolan Richardson, 19
Coach Ortiz, 206
Coach Reese, 38–40
Coach Sowells, 29, 32, 40, 42–43, 68, 69
Coach Stiles, 8
Coach Westerchil, 25, 32, 37, 60, 73
Coburn, Jimmy 106
Cohen, 25–26, 60–61
Colbert, Julian, 58
College, Howard, 24
Collins, 193
   Cecil, 192–93, 195
   Z. 49
Colorado, 24, 61
Comeaux, 29, 69
Conner, Shannon 108, 109
Cooley, Lana, 3
Cooley, Lara, 67

Corbin, 44
Cornelia, 68–69
Cornellli Jackson, 198
Counts, 102
Covington, 104
Cowboys, 13, 19
Cowgirls, 41
Cox, Helen, 47, 67
Cox, Sam LtGen (Ret) 107, 108, 186
Craft, 198
   Bobby, 9–10, 64
Cranson, 130
Crawford, Billy, v–1, 10, 16, 56, 64, 209
Crispin Craft, 202
Crittle, 111, 112
Crosby, 104, 105
CrossCountry, 199
Crow, Jim 12
Crowley, 63
Cryer, Justin, 203-204
Cuba, 187
Cudd, 72
Culbert, 48
Culbreath, Billy 106
Curtis, John, 202

D
Dadriana Ford, 49, 67
Dale Hardwick, ,65
Daniels, 29, 67
Daniel 123
Darion Nabors, 45
Darrion Jaiswal, 45, 58
Daryl Joiner, 59
DaShawn Lewis, 45, 58
Davidson, Angela 30–31, 69
Davis, Michael 130
Deano Brown, 63
Dean, Regina 111,112
Defeated Amite in Consolation game, 71
Defeated Bishop Sullivan, 27, 60
Defeated BTW, 69
Defeated East Ascension, 28, 69
Defeated Glen, 69
Defeated Glen Oaks, 29
Defeated Haughton, 26, 60

Defeated Lee, 60
Defeated Northside, 24, 62
Defeated Port Allen, 19
Defeated Rayne, 62
Defeated Ruston, 23, 69
Defeated Scotlandville, 34, 60, 73
Defeated Scott, 71
Defeated Tara, 46
Defeated West Ouachita, 202
Defeated Winnfield, 71
Defending champion Benton, 199
Def Farmerville, 72
DeGray, 24, 61
   Reggie, 25–26, 53, 59, 61
   Ronnie, 24, 61, 121
DeGray All-State, 61
Demond Mallet, 24–26, 61, 208
Dennis Fetting, 193, 195
Deon, 95
Derek Wright All-State, 60
DeRidder, 2, 13, 201
DESERT STORM, 186
Deshun McNeely, 198
Digital Archives Online, 210
Dionte Kennedy, 40, 59
Discus Thrower Scott Ewes, 198
District Champions, 26, 45, 88, 101, 103, 110–11, 119, 122–29, 152
Dixon, 21–22
   Regina, 21–22, 70, 109, 110
   Richie, 58
Domino, David, 21, 117
Dorsey, Montreal, 24
Dowden, Kim, 22, 112, 114
Dowden, Jill, 109
Downs, 12
Doyal, Hannah, 201
Dry Creek, 4, 66
Dual-sport star Duwon Tolbert, 46
Durrett, 104
Dutchtown, 42, 68
Duwon Tolbert, 46, 58

E
East Beauregard, 13
East Jefferson, 44, 59

Eber Sandell, 65
Edwards, Jimmy, 8, 65, 88
Efosa Evbuomwan, 193
Elber Sandell, 8, 65
Elkins, Chris, 36, 73, 130
Ellender, 67
Ellis, Cathy, 109, 110
Emmy-nominated costume designer, 187
Ennis Flowers, 24, 61–62, 121
Eunice, 27
Europe, 25, 208
Evans, 5, 9
Ewes, 198
   Scott, 199

F
Faith Training Academy, 206
Falero, Ray, 61
Faulkner, Wayne, 6
Faye Jean West, 191
Federal Government, 186
Feliciano, Jacob, 193
Ferguson, Danny, 3
Fertitta, 2
Flowers, Ennis, 119
Football star Bernardo Henry, 198
Football star Kevin Mawae, 206
Ford, Justin, 198
Ford, Shelia 111, 113
Ford, Xavier, 50
Foster 130
Foster Thomas, 14
Frederick, Brian, 102
French, Ricky, 202
Freshley, Robert, 14, 105, 106
   Mark, 109
   Ginny, 22, 112, 113, 114
   John, 20, 103
   LTC Bob, 15
Fulda, Cindy 104
Fulton, Sam 102
Funderburk, 42, 68, 133

G
Gabor, 104
Gaines, 107, 108, 197

Gallashaw, Caleb, 193
Gammage, Percy, 17, 107, 108
Gardiner, W 105
Garland, 112
Gates 125
Gautreaux, 11
Gendron, Joe, 10, 64
Gilbert Field, 4
Gill, 129
Ginny Freshley, 22–23, 69
Girls' Coaches, 56
Girls Record, 105, 108, 111, 139
Glossup, Ann, 113
Goins, Don, 8, 65, 88
Goins, Larry, 65, 85
Gonzalez, 113
Gordon, Vanessa 111, 112
Gormley, 95
Gotreaux, 71
Graduate David Smith, 186
Graduate Tony McDonald, 187
Grambling, 14, 18
Grant Westerchil, 18–19, 34, 53, 55, 60–62
Gray, 112, 114
Green, Kedric 125
Green, Daniel, 34
Green, Jason, 202
Green, Nick, 193
Greenhouse, 67
Grigg, 46, 53, 58
Guidry, 48
  Eric, 48, 67
Guinnell Smart, 8, 53, 56, 71
Gwinn 130

H
Hall, 11, 111, 112, 206
Hall of Fame Coach Charles Smith, 32
Hamilton, Camille, 201
Hammond, 44
Hamm, Jeron 40
Hardwick, 8, 65
  Dale, 8, 65
  Danny, 10, 64
Hardin, 102
Harmon, Johnathon, 204

Harper, 6
Harrington, 136
Harville, Adele, 3
Havana Arts Biennial, 187
Hawkens, 112
Hawkins, Marro 20
Haygood, Cindy, BG, 186
Haymon, Georgia, 84
Hearns, 127
Hearns, Johnnie, 73
Hengstenberg, 9
Henry, Bernardo, 199
Henson, John, 10, 64
Herring, 86
Herzog, 123
Hickerson, 18, 63
Hickman, Eula, 30, 121
Hicks, Wayne, 202
Hicks High School, 206
Hiers, Nikki, 29, 69, 123
High, Lee, 32
High, Vernon, 12, 14
High jumper Anthony Craft, 198
High School Sports Reporter, 206
hired Jordan Andrews, 50
HL Russell, Ph.D. 16
Hoecker, Ashley, 201
Hollean Mathis, 3
Hollifield, 93
Holland, 112, 123
Holly Wentz-Reeves, 208
Holt, Brian, 125
Holt, Terry, 105, 197
Holt, E, 86
Holtsberry, 110
Honor, 208
Hopkins, Jonathan, 34, 36, 73, 198
Hornbeck, 4
Houston, 68, 187
Houston Texans, 44
Howard, 69
  Connie, 22, 70, 111, 112
  Faye 111
  Jerry, 112
  Karen, 23, 114
  Troy, 199

Jon Howerton, 186
Hubert, 22
Hub Jordan, 8, 22, 24, 38, 53–54, 61–62, 70
Hudgens, 127
Hughes, Ken 102
Hunter, Alden 108
Hunter, Aaron, 193
Huntington, 44, 48, 59, 61

I
Iin, 40
Illinois, 208
Istrouma, 38
Istrouma Terrance Blake, 59

J
Jackson, 18, 123, 127
  Leon, 17–18, 108, 197
Jacob, 71
Jacob Mount, 193
Jakayla Collins, 49, 67
Jakiyra Wilson, 51
James, 64
  Pat, 199
JaRielle James, 49
Jayla Burnett, 50, 67
JC Welch, 8, 65
Jeane, Faye, 71, 84, 85
Jeane, Ruben, 193
Jena, 49
Jennings, 63
Jeresun Atkin, 201
Jeron Hamm, 40
Jimbo Pawlik, 197
JJ Joiner, 26–27, 60, 202
J'mani Ingram, 48, 67
John Henry Gamblin, 2
Johnny Pelt All-State, 66
Johnson, 15, 60
  Cedric, 14–15, 18, 63, 197
  Dinah, 109
  Marcus, 34, 36, 38, 59, 73
  Lester, 108
  Michael, 197
  Natasha, 40–41, 68
  Tim, 202

Joiner, 20, 39, 103
  Daryl, 38–39
  Dennis, 14, 73
  JJ 125
  John, 14, 63
  Lawrence 14, 103, 104
  Keith, 14, 17, 107, 108
  Michael, 20, 62, 112
  Oscar, 197
Joiner brothers, 14
Jones, 114
Jones, Damien, 73
Jones, Darrell, 19, 62
Jonesboro, 65
Jordan, 22, 24, 53, 54, 67
  Brandon, 50
  Hubert, 19
Joye Pangelinan, 29
JROTC, 187
Ju'liun Culbert, 50
Judy Porter, 12
Junior Derek Mayo, 202

K
Kadence Reibold, 51
Karsen Kreps, 201
Kavika, 61
Kees, Ralph, 9, 64
Keke Culbert, 48, 67
Kelly, David, 73
Kelly, Roderick, 44
Kemp Tucker, 3
Kennedy, 24, 42, 68, 132
  Pam, 21
  Patrick, 24, 62, 119
  Randy, 18, 19, 62, 110
  Robert 109
  Shonte, 68
  Steve, 18–19, 62, 109, 110,111
Kennedy Smith, 8
Kent State, 187
Kerrigan Small, 49, 67
Kerry, Gerald, 14, 105, 106, 107
Keshera Culbert, 48, 67
Kevin Mawae, 193
Keys, 106, 123, back cover

Khrystian Hoffpauir, 193
Kile, Cheryl, 93
Killeen Texas, 43
Kirk, Tammy, 21
Kirk, Suzanne, 109
Kristi Perkins Won, 67
Kuhlow, Rolf, 197
Kurtina Holland, 30, 69

L

Lafosse, John, 202
LaGrange, 24, 61, 67
Lake, 71
Lake Charles, 46
Lake Charles American Press, 210
Langford, Ronnie, 205
Larrie King, 187
Larry, 8, 39, 59
  Frank, 38–40, 59, 132, 134
Larue, Scott, 21, 24, 62, 117, 119
LaShawn Walters, 44
LaShawn Waters, 59
Last Year, 96
Latham, 64
  James, 10
Laurence, 64
  Steve, 10, 13
Lawton, Keith, 202
Leach, Claude, 187
Leach, Jimmy, 9–10, 64
LeDay, Jade, 50, 67
Lee, 20, 58, 62, 104, 159
Leesville baseball, 202
LEESVILLE BASKETBALL TEAMS, 5
Leesville Boys, 2–3
Leesville Daily Leader, 210
Leesville High, 4, 11–12
Leesville High School, v, 12, 16, 51, 53, 186–87, 193, 209–10
Leesville High School Basketball, v
Leesville High School in Leesville, v
Leesville High School in terms, 43
Leesville High School Yearbooks, 210
Leesville history, 19
Leesville Leader, 2, 34
Leesville Lions Club, 207

Leesville Tournament, 11
Lenahan, (Gautreaux) 11, 96
Levander Liggins, 44, 59
Levon White, 17–18, 63
Lewis, 65
  Mike, 193
LHSAA (Louisiana High School Athletic Association), v, 32, 73, 206
LHSAA Hall of Fame, 206
LHSAA State Meet, 198–99
LHS Boys' Cross Country Team, 199
LHS Principal, 14, 16
  former, 209
LHS Sports Hall, 9, 19, 25, 193, 199, 206, 208
LHS Wampus Cat Football History, 193
LHS Win/Loss Records, 58
LHS yearbooks, 21, 83
Liberty High, 32
Lieutenant General, 186
LIFE Magazine, 186
Liggins, 44, 138, 139
Lindy Porter, 11, 12, 195
Lipton 107
Lonnie, 61
Lorenda Smart, 22
Louise Bonin Lady Cats, 69
Louisiana Christian University, 22
Louisiana College, 9, 12, 22, 29
Louisiana High School Athletic Association. *See* LHSAA
Louisiana-Lafayette, 25
Louisiana National Guard, 186
Louisiana Sports and LHS Hall of Famer, 11
Louisiana Sports Hall, 194, 206
Louisiana State Hall, 32
Louisiana Tech, 34, 44, 209
Loyola, 48, 67
LSU, 19, 193, 206
LSU-Alexandria, 46
LSU star Greg Fontenot, 202
Lucas, Terrell, 45, 58, 149
Lucius, 104
Lynch, 10, 15, 63, 102
  Jerry, 14–15, 18, 197
Lyons, Clayton, 3

M

Macias, Ray, 202
Macphearson, 112
Macklin Mcray, 198
Magee, Haley, 201
Mallet, 14, 22, 25, 61
   Andre, 21
   Demond, 24–26, 61, 121, 208
   Michael, 14, 53, 55, 62–63
   Mike, 18, 70, 209
Malhett, Andrew, 116
Manager Haley McConathy, 201
Manuel, 107
Matthews, 104
Morris, Logan, 73
Maravich, Pete, 206
Marksville, 30, 69
Marro Hawkins signs, 62
Marsh, Tony, 19, 62
Marshle, 112
Martin, 47, 111
   Chelsea, 43, 47, 67, 139
   Amy 123
   Eric 110, 111
Martinez, J, 9
Mason, Walter, 73
Massey, 128
   Kristi 127
   Lewis 65
Massie, Louis, 8
Mastro, 43, 45
   Carl, 53–54
Mastrosimone, 45, 145
   Carl, 43, 58–59
Matthews, Bernard, 197
Mawae, Kevin, 195
Mayeaux, Dennis, 14, 103
   Kay 105
Mayo, 202
   Derek, 204
McAlpin, 72
McChrystal, Mary, 29, 69, 121
McClure, 42, 68
   Regina, 42, 68
McCoy, Nigel, 193
McCray, 125
McCrery, Jim, 187
McCummings, 50, 51
McDaniel, 72
McDonald, 13, 64
   Gary, 10, 13, 64
   Tony, 187
McKenna Goodwin, 201
McLauren, 130
McNeese, 13, 68, 197, 202
McNeese State, 19, 25, 41
McNeese State University Hall of Fame, 208
McQueen, 44, 59
   Darren, 13, 44, 59
   Malachi, 48, 67
McShane, Mike 106
Mechelle Bowman, 199
Menard, 64
Michael, 58
Miller, 68–69, 111
   Cornelia, 29, 43, 53, 123
Mitchell, Ashley, 129, 130
Minden, 50, 67
Miss, Ole, 31
Mississippi State, 69
Miss Stokes, 195
Monroe, 42, 49, 69
Montae Lynch, 193
Montreal Dorsey, 24, 25, 61
Moore, 130
Moore, Aaron, 73
Moore, Thomas, 60
More, Thomas, 62, 69
Murphy, Russell, 14, 105

N

Nabors, 58
NAIA All-American honors, 199
Naismith, 1
NASA's Johnson Space Center, 187
Natchitoches, 23, 38, 69, 206
National Cowboy, 206
National Letter, 47
National Merit Scholarship, 187
National Rodeo, 11

Navy Cross, 186
NBA, 19
NCAA Championships, 208
NCAA Division II Playoff appearance, 13
Neely, Russ 107
Neubert,
  Tom, 202
  Susie, 19
Neville, 48–49, 67, 201
Newman, 128
NFL, 193, 198
Nichols, Jimmie, 2
Nikita Wilson, 17, 62
Nix, 105
Norris, Annette, 84
Northeast Louisiana University (NLU), 20
Northside, 44, 46, 58
Northside Vidall Corbin, 58
Northwestern State, 31–32, 34, 204
Norton, Grady 111
Noel, Robert 14
NSU, 15, 31, 42, 68

O

Oakdale, 63, 65, 71
Oak Grove, 8, 71
Oaks, 69
  Glen, 24, 61
Oklahoma City, 206
Old School, 186
Oliver, Matt, 108
Ontario Agnew, 73
Opelousas, 29, 46, 69, 198
Opelousas Duwon Tolbert, 58
Opelousas Frank Larry, 59
Opelousas, 39
Ortiz,
  Vic 10, 206, 208
  Ray 19
Owen, Charles, 209

P

Paddy, Betty, 8, 72, 84
Pagan, Carlos, 50, 58
Pajinag, Matt, 193

Palmer, 20, 112
Panola Junior College, 22
Paris, Nita, 16, 71, 104
Paris, Ted, 16
Parish, Vernon, 2, 4, 9, 11, 186, 206, 209
Parker, 126, 127, 128, 129
Parker, Ebony, 32, 41, 68
Parkway, 32, 44, 59
Payton, Steve 106
Peabody, 32, 39, 44, 45, 47, 60, 63
Pecan Island High School, 14
Pelt, Johnny, 4
Perkins, Kristi, 49, 57, 67
Peyton Lipps, 193
Pickering, 4,5
Pineville, 13, 41, 61, 63
Sheronda Bowers, 68
Piper Fowler, 51
Pitkin, 4–5
Pittman, Kavika 61
Plaquemine, 46, 58
Ponder Craft, 3
Pope, Brett, 193
Port, 62
Port Barre, 65
Porter, 206, 208
  Cathy, 196
  David,195
  Judy, 11, 196
  Porter girls/sisters, 11, 195
Portland Trailblazers, 19
Poteat, 130
Potter, Christy 130
Potter, Penny 104, 105
Pratt, 105
Preston, Jay, 198
Price, Randy 197
Principal Renita Page, 201

Q

Quarterfinalists, 119
Quick Highlights of Other Great Teams, 193

R

Ragland, 109, 112
Raiford, Patsy, 112
Rand, 6
Red Beeson, 2
Reese, 9, 12, 40
   Richard, 9, 25, 53, 55, 63–65, 95
   Tracy, 38, 59
   Michael (back cover)
Reeves, 199
Reibold, 51
Reggie, 61
Rhodes, 71
   Eric, 20, 62
Richard Schwarts State scoring, 64
Richard Schwartz set, 9
Rich History of Leesville High School, 186
Richwood, 62
Riddle, Garland, 187
Rim, Marcus, 40, 136
Roberson, Victor, 197
Robert, 20, 62–63, 67, 197
Robert Causey, 193
Robinson, Homer, 3
Robinson, Telia 129
Rock, James, 14, 106, back cover
Rodeo Hall of Fame, 206
Roebuck, 84
Rogers, 67
   Linda, 48, 67
Rolon, Roger, 117
Rone, Greg 193
Ron Guidry's World Series, 206
Rosepine, 4–5
Rowzee
   Fred 2
   Daniel, 111, 112
Rural schools, 11
Russell, H. Lynn, Ph.D. 16, 209
Ruston, 23, 38

S
Saints, 47
Salisbury, Robert, 20, 62
Salmen, 32, 34, 60
Sam Houston, 42
Sandell, Elber 85

Saunders, 104
Saunders, Donna, 16
Sawyer, Darius, 193
Schools James Williams, 14
Schwartz, Richard, 9, 64, 209
Sciabarassi, 50, 57, 67
Scoggins, Susan, 21, 108, 109
Scogin, Joy Ann 84
Seastrunk, Ronald, 110, 111
Seginald, 58
Seginald Bryant, 46
Self, Angela 21
Selma, Malcom, 39
Semi Finals, 71–72
Senda Berenson, 1
Sepi Toga, 32, 68
Sepulveda, 58
   Carlos, 46
Sexson-Peters, Summer, 48
Sexson, 9, 129
Severino 130
Shaquille O'Neal, 206
Shaw, 20, 62, 112
   Ricky, 202
Shelton, 63
Sheppard, 136
Shermaine Jones, 193
Sheronda Bowers, 32, 40–41, 68
Shonte Kennedy, 42, 68
Shonte Kennedy All-State, 68
Shreve, 69
Shreveport, 44, 49
Shreveport Journal, 210
Shreveport Times, 210
Shyann McCummings, 50, 51, 67
Sig Milerski, 193
signed National Letters, 29
Singleton, Marcus, 39, 130
Skidmore, 106, 107
Skinner, Asa, 10, 64
Skinner, Clint 125
Slidell, 34
Small, 49
Smart, John, 102
Smart, Lorenda, 112, 113
Smith, 103, 112, 198, 210

Aaron, 26
Calvin, 109
Danny, 193
Denzel, 3
Dustin, 125, 202, 204
Erin, 42, 68, 128
included, 198
Randall, 14, 63, 103
Raymond, 14, 104
Smith College, 1
Smith, Randal 14
Smith, Catfish 14
Societal Change, 12
South Beauregard, 67
Sowells, 53
Joe, 29, 43, 53, 56, 68–69
Space Center, 187
Sparks,
Darrel, 112
Francis, 109,199
Regina, 21
Terry, 197
Special Section, 193
Spriggs, 149
Springfield, 1
Stanley, Finley, 3
Stanley, Garland, 3
Star Richard Reese, 19
State Semi-Finalists, 62, 71, 113, 117, 152
State Semi Finals, 58
St. Clergy, Jesse, 201
Stephens, Kay, 21
Stewart, 2, 104
Bruce, 202
Stewart's squad, 2
St. Joseph, 71
St. Louis, 47
St. Martinville, 38, 59
St. Michael, second round, 45
Stokes, 195
Judy, 195–96
Stone, 186
Strait, Debbie, 16, 104
St Thomas Moore, 34, 73, 25, 68
St. Thomas Moore, 73
Sulphur, 69

Summer Sexton Peters, 53
Summers, 130
Super Bowls, 206
Super Dome, 193
Superintendent, 9, 14
Suzette Kuhlow Kent, 186
Swain, Eunice, 3
Symons, Rod 106

T
Tajai McCollum, 201
Talbert, Milton, 3
Talyn Adams, 193
Tangie Riley, 27–28, 30, 69
Taylor, Kay, 70, 108
Taylor, Julie, 108, 109
T-Berry, 206
Teague, Nicholas, 199
Teal 127
Ted Castillo, 187, 206, 208
Tekeirah Harris, 50, 67
Temple, 8, 9, 53, 72
Junior, 10, 64
Temple State Runner, 72
Tennis, 205
Terrance, 59
Teurlings Catholic, 201
Texas, 48
Texas A&M, 13
Texas Highway, 4
Thibodeaux, Quintella 129
Thomas, 29, 61, 68–69, 198, 114, 127
Angie, 23, 69
Garland, 110
Lonnie, 25–26, 61
Natasha, 41
Tracey, 29, 69
Viola, 30–32, 69
Thurman, Marcus, 202
Tiamaree Root, 205
Timbelake, 54
Tinsley, 102, 105
Tied, 120, 126
Tiffy Clifton, 29
Tigers, 19
Timberlake, Josh, 58

Tim Lynch, 10, 64
Tinsley, Floyd, 63
Tinsley, Kathy, 16, 104
Tinsley, Mose, 12
Tinsley Tracy 14
Tioga, 61, 71
Title IX, 16
Tolbert, 46
Tonga, 127
Tori Daniels, 29, 69
Total, 54, 56
Tracey Thomas Both, 69
Track and Field, 197
Track Team, 18, 198
Transition, 9
Travis, 18
  Eric, 18, 63, 108, 109, 110
  Neal, 20, 62
  Steve, 18, 62, 110, 111
  Vernon, 17
Trevino, 114
Truax, 85
Tulane, 29, 69
Tulsa University, 19
Turner, Richard 107
Two-Time All-State, 204
Tying Frank Larry, 47
Tying Gary McDonald, 59
Tyler Junior College, 46
Tyshawn Johnson, 44

U
ULM, 42, 68
Undefeated District Champs, 63
United States, 12, 186
United States Air Force, 186, 209
United States Army, 186
Upshaw, Cordell, 14, 105, 130
Upshaw, Dexter, 14
Upshaw, Cedric, 18, 109
US Army, 2
US Congressmen, 187
US government, 12, 187
US Navy, 206
US service academies, 187

V
Valedictorian, 206
Vandine, D, 14, 103
Vernia, 71
Vernia Gautreaux (Lenahan), 11
Vernon High School, 14, 53
Vernon Parish Annual School Rally, 4
Vernon Parish Library, 210
Vernon Parish Rally, 4
Vernon's doors, 12
Vidall Corbin, 44, 59
Vietnam War, 186
Viola, 68–69

W
Walker, 30, 63
Wallace, 47
  Tiffany, 43, 47, 67–68.138, 139, 141
Wallace signs, 67
Walker,102
Walters, 102
Wampus Cat Baseball Team, 204–5
Wampus Cat Marching Band, 187
Wampus Cats, 193, 206
Ward, 193
Washington-Marion, 58
Watson, Chris, 39
Weisgerber, 11
Wentz, Holly, 111, 199
West, 114
Westerchil, 19, 25, 37–38, 53, 7, 73,111
  Beth, 210
  Joe, 25
  Western Heritage Museum, 206
West, Vicki, 105
West Monroe, 29
Wheaton College, 199, 208
White, Levon 108
White, Zack, 24
Whittaker, Gwendolyn, 8, 71, 85, 88
Windham, 105
Williams, 201
Wilson, 18–19, 51, 58
  Carlton, 105
  Deandre, 46–47
  Gabriel, 73

    Jamal, 26, 60, 125
    Nikita, 18–19, 62–63, 109, 110, 111
    Nya, 30
Winnsboro, 8, 71
WL Bynog, 202
Wofford, 61
Wofford University, 25
Woodlawn, 49, 60, 67, 73
Woodruf, 104
Woods, 34, 36, 38, 59, 113, 114
    Eric, 32, 34, 38, 60, 73
    Matthew, 110, 111
Woods All-State, 59
Wooley, Norma, 3
Worfel, 104
World Champion, 206
World War II, 2
Wossman, 24, 61
Wright, 27, 114
    Derek, 27, 60, 125, 127

Y
YA Title, 206
Year-by-Year, 58
Year Honor, 40
Yepez, Miguel, 24, 62
Young, Colleen, 11, 96

Z
Zinger, Keith, 191
Zolon Stiles, 8, 66

[